DECORATIVE PAINTING

PAINTING

Baby Animal

TREASURES

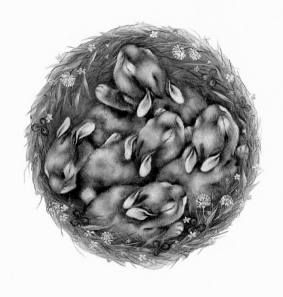

PEGGY HARRIS

NORTH LIGHT BOOKS
CINCINNATI, OHIO

For my mother, La, the first decorative painter in my life;
my father, Neal, who taught me the joys of nature;
and Bernie Kennedy, friend, decorative painter, teacher and mentor.

Painting Baby Animal Treasures. Copyright © 1999 by Peggy Harris. Manufactured in China. All rights reserved. The patterns and drawings in this book are for the personal use of the decorative painter. By permission of the author and publisher, they may be either hand-traced or photocopied to make single copies, but under no circumstances may they be resold or republished. It is permissable for the purchaser to paint the designs contained herein and sell them at fairs, bazaars and craft shows. No other part of this book may be reproduced in any form or by any electronic or mechanical means including information storage and retrieval systems without permission in writing from the publisher, except by a reviewer, who may quote brief passages in a review. Published by North Light Books, an imprint of F&W Publications, Inc., 1507 Dana Avenue, Cincinnati, Ohio 45207. (800) 289-0963. First edition.

Other fine North Light Books are available from your local bookstore, art supply store or direct from the publisher.

03 02 01 00 99   5 4 3 2 1

Library of Congress Cataloging-in-Publication Data

Harris, Peggy
    Painting baby animal treasures / Peggy Harris.—1st ed.
       p.   cm.
    Includes index.
    ISBN 0-89134-944-8
    ISBN 0-89134-909-X (pbk.)
    1. Animals in art. 2. Animals—Infancy—Pictorial works. 3. Painting—Technique.
  I. Title.
ND1380.H36 1999
751.45'432—dc21
                                          98-48509
                                             CIP

Editors: Dawn Korth and Kathy Kipp
Production editors: Amy Jeynes and Christine Doyle
Production coordinator: Erin Boggs

Photo by Tommy Lawson

About the Artist

Peggy Harris was born in Washington, DC, grew up in Kansas City and graduated from the University of Kansas. Peggy and her husband, Bob Sanders, live in the wooded hills of Nashville, Tennessee, surrounded by the wildlife and pets that inspire her work.

"The Harris Method" began over twenty years ago when Peggy began experimenting with nontraditional painting techniques and materials, searching for a way to supply the demand for her paintings. Not only did Peggy's new method enable her to create literally thousands of paintings herself, but, incredibly, it was teachable!

Today, "Peggy Harris's Paintable Kingdom," a production of WDCN-Nashville, is enjoyed nationwide on public television. Students flock to Peggy's workshops and seminars so they too can learn to create realistic fur and feathers in a modicum of time. Thousands have read and benefited from Peggy's first book, *Painting Baby Animals With Peggy Harris*, and her videotape *Painting Baby Animals* from North Light Books.

Now, Peggy invites you to join her as she combines two lifelong passions, baby animals and decorative painting. It's the best of both worlds.

Come share the love!

Table of Contents

Share the Love

At last! A foolproof, fun, fast way to paint amazingly realistic fur and feathers on deco-  rative surfaces! Peggy Harris has made her basic, systematic method for painting animals even easier, so you too can create baby animals that not only will touch your heart, but that you'll want to reach out and touch!

Even beginners can create adorable, lifelike, three-dimensional, beautifully shaded baby animals. Experienced painters will be fasci- nated with the speed and effortlessness with which they can paint animals using Peggy's techniques.

Join Peggy as she shows you step-by-step how to use acrylic or oil paints and gel medi- ums, Q-tips and cotton balls, and a stiff bristle brush to create decorative painting heirlooms: baby animals to paint now and baby animals to cherish for generations to come!

Projects

MATERIALS

A limited palette of oil or acrylic paints and mediums, a few brushes, everyday "fluff stuff" and some basic materials you probably already have are all you'll need to paint these baby animal projects.

Since you are buying less, buy better—especially brushes! Only professional-quality brushes produce beautiful fur and fine detail. Some brands of materials have properties well-suited to this technique. You may want to compare your supplies to those used to create the baby animals in this book.

1. **Surfaces**—glass, metal, slate or wood

2. **Surface preparation supplies**—vinegar, fine-grit sandpaper, J.W. etc. Professional Wood Filler, J.W. etc. White Lightning or First Step wood sealer, tack cloth, gesso (optional), synthetic #0000 steel wool pad, piece of brown paper bag

3. **Acrylic paint**—for base coat, undercoat and background

4. **Transfer materials**—mechanical pencil or stylus, tracing paper, grey or white graphite paper, stencil blank for stenciled background shapes

5. **Scotch Magic Tape**

6. **Krylon #1311 Matte Finishing Spray**

7. **Container**—for water or thinner

8. **Small palette**—such as a cut-down plastic lid from a Q-tips box for oils or a small Masterson Sta-Wet Palette for acrylics

9. **Palette knife**—small painting knife

10. **Brushes**—Professional-quality synthetic hair, sable and white-bristle brushes. Ruby Satin (synthetic hair) and Grand Prix (natural white bristle) brushes

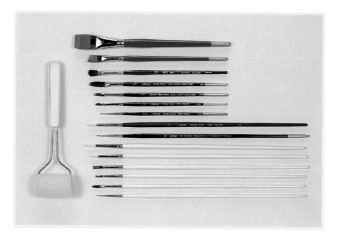

from Silver Brush, Ltd. give excellent performance in both oil and acrylic. Renaissance, Golden Natural, Wee Mop and Ultra Mini series from Silver Brush are also recommended.

You need at least one of each type:
- tiny hair round (#0 or smaller)
- small hair bright (#1)
- medium hair bright (#2, #3)
- small stiff round bristle brush (#1)
- medium stiff round bristle brush (#2)
- large stiff round bristle brush (#4 or #5—used for Project 10 only)
- small synthetic filbert grass comb (rake)—Ruby Satin ⅛-inch and ¼-inch preferred
- small mop brush (optional but very useful)
- sponge and flat brushes for base-coating and backgrounds
- ⅜-inch angled synthetic for undercoating

Also: various flats and specialty brushes for decorative painting techniques

11. **Gel**—for oils: Res-n-gel Non-Toxic Oil Painting Medium by Martin/F. Weber preferred. Thickened linseed oil may be substituted for gel medium, but it requires some technique adjustment.
    Gel—for acrylics: Plaid/FolkArt Blending Gel Medium. A slow-drying acrylic gel is essential.

12. **Oil paints**—Professional Permalba Artists Oil Color
    - Titanium or Permalba White
    - Ivory Black
    - Raw Umber
    - Cadmium Yellow Light
    - Burnt Sienna
    - Sap Green
    - Vermilion Permanent
    - Prussian Blue

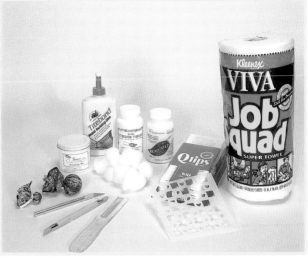

13. **Oil painting mediums**—Turpenoid or Turpenoid Natural turpentine substitute or odorless thinner, RapiDry Quick Drying Oil Medium (optional)

14. **Acrylic paints**—All are Plaid/Folk Art Artists' Pigment except as noted
    - Titanium White
    - Wicker White (FolkArt Acrylic Color)
    - Warm White
    - Medium Yellow
    - Portrait
    - Red Light
    - Napthol Crimson
    - True Burgundy
    - Burnt Sienna
    - Raw Umber
    - Sap Green
    - Hauser Green Light
    - Hauser Green Medium
    - Hauser Green Dark
    - Green Umber
    - Prussian Blue
    - Pure Black

15. **Acrylic paint mediums (optional):**
    - Plaid/FolkArt Floating Medium
    - Plaid/FolkArt Extender for Acrylic Paint

16. **Glycerin emollient**—generic drug store brand. Add a few drops in the palette to most acrylic gel mediums to extend the open (drying) time.

17. **"Fluff Stuff"**
    - Soft, heavy paper towels such as Kleenex Viva or Job Squad
    - Chesebrough-Pond's Q-tips Cotton Swabs, 300 count or more
    - "Cotton" balls (plastic-bagged synthetic "cosmetic puffs," 100 count)

- Silk or nylon cotton ball covers (small squares of old scarf or silky nylon hose to hold cotton balls) and twisty ties

18. **X-Acto knife**—with a #11 blade

19. **Snow spattering tool (optional)**

20. **Stencil for spacing designs (optional)**

21. **Lift-out tool (optional)**

22. **Finishing supplies**—J.W. etc. Right-Step water-base satin varnish or J.W. etc. exterior varnish, wood glue, J.W. etc. Painter's Finishing Wax, synthetic #0000 steel wool pad to apply wax

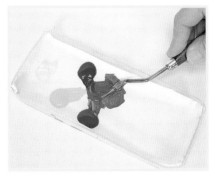

If your project requires a large amount of a color, mix what you'll need ahead of time and store in small airtight containers. Here, I'm mixing my favorite bunny brown.

Little oil paint is needed to paint baby animals. Here, I'm moistening my brush with gel, located in the center of the palette.

MIXING YOUR COLORS

These are approximate formulas based on Professional Permalba Artists Oil Colors and Plaid/FolkArt Artists' Pigment acrylic colors. Squeeze out a "chocolate chip" of each paint. Begin with the first color listed and cautiously add the others. Your mixtures may differ, so always match your colors to the pictures. Check acrylic colors *after* they are dry.

Soft Brown

OIL
4 parts Raw Umber
2 parts Burnt Sienna
1 part Cadmium Yellow Light

ACRYLIC
3 parts Medium Yellow
1 part True Burgundy
1 part Hauser Green Dark

Light Brown

OIL
1 part Cadmium Yellow Light
1 part Raw Umber

ACRYLIC
4 parts Medium Yellow
1 part True Burgundy
1 part Hauser Green Dark

Fawn

OIL
1 part Cadmium Yellow Light
1 part Raw Umber—scant
1 part Burnt Sienna—scant
Vary with yellow

ACRYLIC
5 parts Medium Yellow
1 part True Burgundy
1 part Hauser Green Dark
Vary with yellow

Basic Green

OIL
2 parts Sap Green
1 part Raw Umber
Vary with yellow, white, black
or Prussian Blue

ACRYLIC
2 Parts Raw Umber
1 part Sap Green
1 touch Medium Yellow
Vary with yellow, white, black
or Prussian Blue

Bright Red

OIL
Vermilion Permanent
Vary with yellow

ACRYLIC
Red Light
Vary with yellow

Pink

OIL
1 part Permalba or Titanium White
2 touches Vermilion Permanent

ACRYLIC
1 part Titanium White
2 touches Red Light

Deep Peach

OIL
1 part Permalba or Titanium White
2 touches Vermilion Permanent
1 touch Cadmium Yellow Light
1 touch Raw Umber
Vary with white

ACRYLIC
1 part Portrait
1 touch Napthol Crimson
Vary with white

Basic Blue-Grey

OIL
8 parts Permalba or Titanium White
4 parts Ivory Black
1 part Prussian Blue
Vary with black and white

ACRYLIC
3 parts Titanium White
2 parts Prussian Blue
2 parts Pure Black
1 touch Raw Umber
Vary with black and white

Deep Blue-Black

OIL
4 parts Ivory Black
1 part Prussian Blue

ACRYLIC
4 parts Pure Black
1 part Prussian Blue

Egg Blue

OIL
4 parts Permalba or Titanium White
3 touches Raw Umber
1 touch Ivory Black
1 touch Prussian Blue
1 touch Sap Green
Vary with white

ACRYLIC
1 part Titanium White
3 touches Raw Umber
1 touch Pure Black
1 touch Prussian Blue
1 touch Sap Green
Vary with white

25 TERMS TO KNOW

1. *Airplane*—To lift off or onto the painting surface with the Q-tip or paintbrush, gradually and smoothly, as if the brush were an airplane and the surface the runway.

2. *Base coat*—The water-based paint applied to the prepared surface of the project before design transfer and decorative painting.

3. *Bright brush*—A type of brush with a flat ferrule and a square, chiseled-looking tip. In this book, refers only to a sable or synthetic-hair brush.

4. *Bristle brush*—In this book, refers to a stiff, round bristle brush of either natural or synthetic bristles.

5. *Dirt (Dirty)*—Unwanted paint deposited in white areas of the surface by lift-out tools. Also, paint that has accumulated in these tools and is apt to be redeposited in unwanted areas.

6. *Double-load (Triple-load)*—To paint with two or three colors side by side in a brush.

7. *Dry Q-tip*—A fresh Q-tip that has no thinner, water or paint in it.

8. *Fall off (Flow off) the brush*—To allow thinned paint to flow from the brush to the painting surface without letting the hairs of the brush touch the underlying paint or the surface.

9. *Gel*—A gel-like acrylic or oil medium that transparentizes paint and retains brushstrokes of fur. Res-n-gel Non-Toxic by Martin/F. Weber for oils and FolkArt Blending Gel Medium by Plaid for acrylic paint are preferred. Substitutions may require some alteration of technique.

10. *Glow*—Wet-glow: To create the illusion of light on an area by lifting out paint with a wet Q-tip or brush. Dry-glow: To create a subtler highlight area by lifting out paint with a dry Q-tip.

11. *Lift out*—To remove paint from the painting surface with a Q-tip or brush.

12. *Open time*—The amount of time paint will stay wet and workable before it dries.

13. *Puddle*—To let a droplet of paint flow from the brush onto the middle of a shape and then stretch it to the correct size and shape by stirring it with the brush.

14. *Rake*—In this book, refers to a filbert (oval-tipped) synthetic brush with thin hair used to paint hair or grass. Also called a grass comb.

15. *Re-brush*—To perfect a previously brushed area of fur with a bristle brush. Usually refers to brushing an area that has been glowed.

16. *Rotation (of fur)*—Brushing fur in an orderly sequence of angles as it radiates from a central point.

17. *Rough-brush*—To brush layers of fur on an image using a bristle brush or rake to blend the paint pattern.

18. *Round brush*—A type of brush that has a round ferrule and a pointed tip. Comes in both hair and bristle brushes.

19. *Scrumble*—An invented word meaning a "scruffy-jumble" of paint used in the paint pattern. Implies squiggly strokes, loosely applied.

20. *Snowplow*—To destroy the effect of delicate fur tips by brushing excess paint into the tips. Results from not airplaning the brush.

21. *Stipple (Splat)*—To tap the bristle brush rapidly with the brush held perpendicular to the surface. "Splat" implies stippling with hard hits that cause the bristles to splay.

22. *Travel color*—To allow color accumulated in the bristle brush while brushing fur to be deposited in unwanted areas.

23. *Undercoat*—In this book, to paint the design area inside the largest outline with solid white acrylic paint—usually feathered on fur edges. More than one coat may be needed.

24. *Wet brush*—A small- or medium-sized bright hair brush that has been dipped in water or thinner and squeezed out or wiped clean, but still retains enough moisture to lift out paint from the surface.

25. *Wet Q-tip*—A Q-tip that has been dipped in water or thinner and then blotted on a paper towel pad.

PREPARING SURFACES

A well-prepared surface is the foundation for a project you'll cherish for years to come. Take extra care to give your baby animals a surface they'll be proud to call home.

If you are a new decorative painter, you may wish to seek more detailed preparation information in books devoted to the subject. Those of you who are experienced may have your own special tricks and techniques you prefer to use.

What You'll Need

Here is a basic list of supplies you'll need to prepare and finish most surfaces. Check individual projects for specific materials used.

- Soft paper towels
- Vinegar
- Fine-grit sandpaper
- Wood filler
- Water-based wood sealer
- Tack cloth
- Gesso (optional)
- Synthetic #0000 steel wool pad
- Pieces of heavy brown paper bag for smoothing
- Sponge brush or large, flat synthetic-hair brushes
- Water basin and plastic containers
- Water-based or polyurethane satin varnish—interior and/or exterior
- Wood glue
- Finishing wax

Preparing Glass, Metal and Slate

These are the easiest surfaces because they require little preparation. Just wipe clean with a soft paper towel and diluted vinegar and you're ready to paint. If desired, slate can be sealed with wood sealer to prevent excessive absorption of acrylic paints.

Preparing Wood

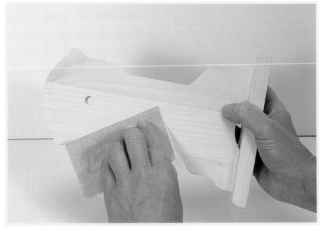

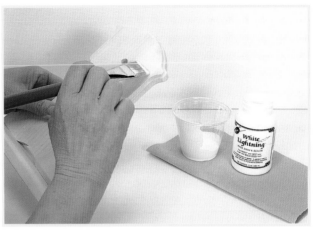

1 Begin by filling any imperfections in your surface with wood filler following label directions. When the filler is dry, sand the entire surface with fine sandpaper (a sanding block or electric sander may help). Remove sanding dust with a tack cloth.

2 Apply an appropriate water-based wood sealer to every surface of the object, even the bottom. This blocks moisture from entering the piece in the future. Sealing raises the wood's grain, so be sure to smooth the surface with a piece of heavy brown paper or lightly sand again and wipe clean with a tack cloth.

3 For even smoother surfaces, apply gesso according to label instructions. You may use one or many coats of gesso. Even inferior surfaces can be brought up to standard with gesso. Lightly sand and dust with a tack cloth between every coat for a really smooth painting surface.

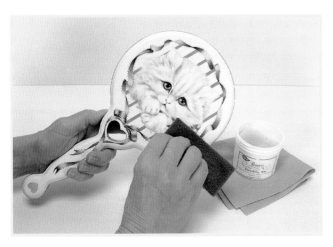

Finishing Your Painted Surface

You've painted a beautiful project, so give it the finish it deserves! Several coats of satin varnish (carefully applied and rubbed down with a brown bag between each coat) will breathe life into your baby animals. Fur will gleam and colors will be more beautiful than when they were painted.

NOTE: In this technique, *never* sand or smooth between the first and second coats of varnish. You could damage the delicate raised fur and feather lines.

Follow the varnish with a coat or two of finishing wax, and you've created an heirloom!

PREPARING TO PAINT

Base-Coating Your Surface

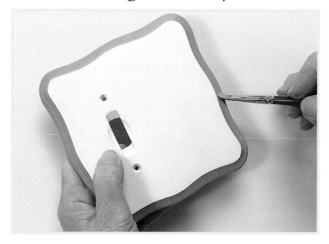

Base-coat your surface with acrylic paint, even if you plan to paint the design in oil.

Use either a sponge brush or a large, flat synthetic brush to apply several thin coats of paint rather than one heavy coat. Smooth between each coat with a piece of brown paper bag and wipe with a tack cloth. A small angled brush is good for painting odd places or colored borders.

Mist the finished base coat with Krylon #1311 Matte Finishing Spray to protect the surface from dirt and stray paint smudges.

What You'll Need

- Soft paper towels
- Acrylic paint for base coat
- Sponge brush or large, flat synthetic brush for base coating
- Water basin
- #0000 synthetic steel wool pad or piece of heavy brown paper bag
- Tack cloth
- Krylon #1311 Matte Finishing Spray
- White and grey transfer paper
- White acrylic paint for undercoating
- Angled brush for undercoating
- Tracing paper
- Mechanical pencil or stylus
- Scotch Magic Tape

Undercoating Your Design

Transfer the outline of the design using white graphite paper when possible. With an angled brush, fill in the outline with several coats of white acrylic paint.

Completely opaque coverage is not necessary except in areas that will be white in the finished design. The angled brush allows you to feather the fur edges slightly as you undercoat. Try not to leave any ridges on the other edges either. Lightly sand with synthetic steel wool or smooth with a brown paper bag.

Surfaces that are base-coated with very pale color may need undercoating only in white and glow areas of the design. However, a thin overall undercoat may be necessary if the surface is too slick because of the acrylic matte spray on the base coat.

TRANSFERRING YOUR DESIGN

Trace black lines and around black shapes

Only indicate or freehand

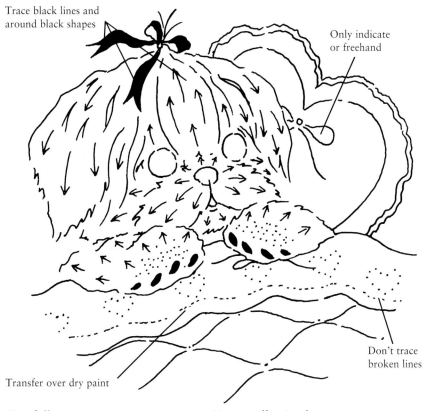

Transfer over dry paint

Don't trace broken lines

Carefully trace your painting pattern. Very small animals quickly become misshapen by the slightest mis-tracing. Even on large animal designs, the eyes are especially vulnerable to distortion. Enlarge or reduce the traced pattern according to the instructions on each pattern page.

Using the Design Patterns in This Book

Decide ahead of time what parts of a design pattern you need to trace. Since you are painting, not drawing, you needn't transfer every detail of a pattern. Usually, dotted lines are painting guidelines and should not be traced.

Trace most solid lines, but transfer only enough parts of these lines to enable you to paint accurately. The fewer transfer marks you have to cope with, the better. Small details, such as grasses, may be indicated only for placement or may be done freehand.

Trace, but don't transfer, elements that will be covered over with paint. Wait and transfer these details onto the dry painting later.

Place your tracing on the surface and secure it with tape. Slip transfer paper under the tracing and re-trace the design. Check early on to make sure the lines are transferring adequately. If your lines are too dark or smudgy, wipe the back of the transfer paper with a soft paper towel before continuing. Be careful not to dent soft wood surfaces by using too much pressure.

PROJECT COLORS

These formulas use Plaid/FolkArt Artists' Pigment acrylic colors (and one FolkArt Acrylic color, Wicker White) for the base coats, backgrounds and decorations in the projects in this book. You may prefer to use similar pre-mixed colors on your surfaces.

Project 2

CREAM SURFACE
30 parts Warm White
1 part Medium yellow—scant
1 part Raw Umber—scant

Project 3

LIGHT BLUE-GREY SURFACE
25 parts Titanium White
1 part Prussian Blue
1 part Pure Black
1 part Raw Umber—scant

Project 5

WHITE SURFACE
Warm White

PALE PEACHY PINK SURFACES
3 parts Warm White
1 part Portrait

Project 6

WHITE SURFACES
Wicker White (FolkArt Acrylic)

BLUE-GREY STRIPES AND BACKGROUND
15 parts Titanium White
1 part Prussian Blue
1 part Pure Black
1 touch Raw Umber

Project 8

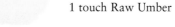

LIGHT CREAM SURFACE
1 part Warm White
1 touch Medium Yellow
1 touch Raw Umber

PEACHY PINK FLOWERS
2 parts Warm White
1 part Portrait
1 touch Napthol Crimson

DEEP PEACH FLOWER CENTERS
1 part Portrait
1 touch Napthol Crimson

PALE PEACHY PINK STRIPING
3 parts Warm White
1 part Portrait

Project 9

DEEP PEACH SURFACE
1 part Portrait
1 part Napthol Crimson

MUSTARD SURFACE
1 part Medium Yellow
1 touch True Burgundy
1 touch Hauser Green Dark
1 touch Napthol Crimson
1 touch Titanium White
1 touch Portrait

Project 10

DEEP BLUE-GREY SURFACE
10 parts Titanium White
3 parts Pure Black
3 parts Prussian Blue
2 parts Raw Umber—scant

DEEP BLUE-BLACK GLAZING
4 parts Pure Black
1 part Prussian Blue

ESSENTIAL TIPS

The projects in this book can be painted in either oil or acrylic paints or even a combination of the two, as long as oil is always *over* acrylic, never under it. Properly executed, the results of oil and acrylic will look identical. Along the way, however, they each have their own idiosyncrasies, advantages and disadvantages you need to be aware of before painting.

For Oil Painters

Painting baby animals with oils on surfaces is even faster and easier than painting on canvas, but a little different. The slick surface of the object you'll be painting is a decided asset when combined with this unique fur technique. Here are some suggestions that may help you:

- Always paint gel over the entire area of the pattern to be painted before you begin.
- *Use little to no pressure* on brushes! Everything is slick—the surface, the gel, the oil paint. Manipulate the sliding paint with a feather touch. Too much pressure and you'll scoop the paint off the surface.
- Continue brushing and working. Just as you think you've made a mess, the gorgeous fur appears like magic. This usually happens in the glow-and-re-brush stage when the perfect combination of paint and gel are now riding on the surface. Clean and re-gel your brush often in this stage.
- Tickle your animal with a small mop brush! You'll be amazed at how quickly already-brushed fur can look even better with this technique. No pressure—lots of air-swooshing!
- Dry-Q-tip and dry-brush glowing may be sufficient to obtain luminous fur. Wait and see before proceeding to wet-glowing.
- Some surfaces can be awkward to work on, and it's easy to accidentally get your hand in your wet painting. This is when you'll wish oils dried like acrylics! You may find it convenient to work on smaller areas of the pattern at a time.
- Use Res-n-gel Non-Toxic, pale drying oil or some Copal varnish mixed with your paint for projects that can't be varnished later (such as frosted Christmas balls, where a final coat of varnish would remove the frosting). The paint will retain a satin sheen when dry.

For Acrylic Painters

Painting baby animals with acrylics is easy as long as you are knowledgeable and vigilant about open times and don't paint more than you can finish before the paint dries. Here are some pointers to insure your success:

- Not all acrylic paints and gels are equal in this technique. Choose paints and gel that have the greatest open time.
- Acrylic gel is best kept in a small, separate container, as it tends to "melt" into a wet palette.
- Paint more gel under the paint pattern than you use in other methods.
- Experiment with glycerin proportions in your gel and note open time variations.
- Keep a small area of wet gel painted just ahead of where you are working to insure proper blending as you move into the new area.
- *Paint and finish small areas at a time*, moving in an orderly fashion to successive areas. The pictures in this book show each step as it appears over the *entire* body of the animal. *You* should work only a small part of the animal (such as an ear or hip) at a time, proceeding through all the steps of paint, brush, glow, re-brush and finish on that part. Then, move to an adjacent part of the animal and begin the steps over again—paint, brush, glow, re-brush and finish.
- Quickly brush edge fur to a finished stage after painting the paint pattern in the part you are working on. Edge fur dries rapidly when it hits the base coat of the surface.
- Interior fur will stay workable longer if you frequently replenish the gel in your brush while you brush the fur. Drying interior areas can also be wetted down and re-brushed with plenty of gel.
- If an area does dry too soon, let it cure sufficiently before continuing to prevent surprise lifting. Then, overpaint and begin again, or try some glazing techniques—a real acrylic plus!
- Sometimes paint can't be varnished later, such as on a frosted Christmas ball, where varnish would remove the frosting. To get a satin sheen in such situations, try mixing some gloss varnish into the paint—or experiment with acrylic enamels.
- Use whatever floating, blending, stroke and loading techniques you've already mastered (but which are not discussed in this book) to produce exquisite finish work around your baby animals.

LIFTING OUT PAINT

Lifting out paint is a quick and effective method for achieving glowing, shining fur, brilliant highlights and the illusion of three-dimensional shapes. Sometimes lifting out wet paint to expose the background surface creates other elements of the design, such as a ruffle or a blade of grass. Good lifting-out technique also enables you to endlessly change or fix your wet painting—the ultimate eraser!

Q-tip Positions

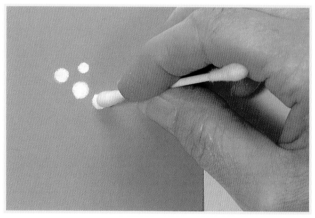

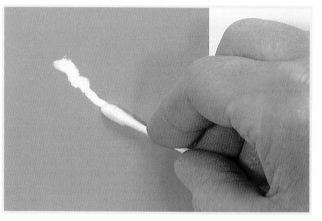

The Q-tip Straight Up Holding the Q-tip like a pencil and perpendicular to the painting surface creates round shapes such as bubbles. Spiral the Q-tip in ever larger concentric circles to enlarge the shape.

The Q-tip on the Side Grasp the Q-tip with all four fingers along its stem to create all other shapes. Using the Q-tip on its side is the most frequent and versatile position.

Q-tip Adjustment

Dry and wet Q-tips may sometimes need to be adjusted in size and tightness.

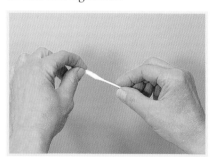

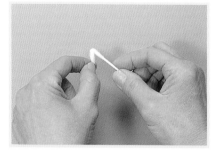

1 Hold the tip steady in one hand and, with a slight jiggling motion, pull the stem away from the tip to loosen part of the cotton on the tip of the Q-tip.

2 Resist the temptation to pull off the loosened cotton. Instead, place it back along the stem.

3 Push the Q-tip up between your thumb and forefinger, twisting as you push, until it is tight. You've made your first custom Q-tip!

Lifting Out Shapes

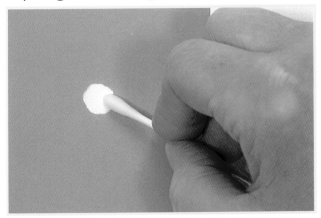

1 Using a Q-tip on its side, begin in the middle of a shape and gradually enlarge it. When using a wet Q-tip, always lightly jiggle it in place to release some water or thinner onto the paint.

2 Use less pressure on the Q-tip as you approach the edge of a shape. With dry Q-tips, this creates a haze. With wet Q-tips, it creates a mushy paint ring essential to further blending.

Wet Q-tip Skills

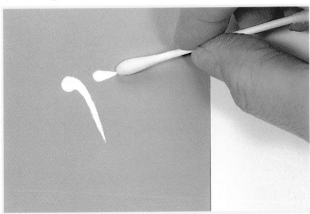

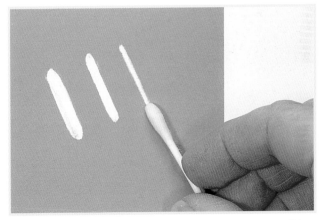

Airplaning Jiggle a wet and tightened Q-tip on its side to make a shape. With evenly decreasing pressure, airplane the Q-tip off the surface. As you lift off, you can create an ever-thinner line.

Varying Widths The same Q-tip can create many lift-out widths. Vary your pressure to create wide and medium lift-outs. No pressure on the Q-tip creates very thin lift-outs, since only a tiny area of the rounded shape touches the surface.

Basic Keys to Lifting Out Paint

Use clean lift-out tools. Once a tool has paint in it, it acts as a loaded brush and redeposits paint ("dirt") onto your surface. Clean your brush or change to a clean side of your cotton ball frequently. Use Q-tips by the fistful to prevent the inclination to use a "dirty" one.

Use light pressure. Paint easily lifts off slick surfaces. Very light pressure on your lift-out tool results in finer, more delicate work. Use evenly increasing or decreasing pressures for smooth airbrushed-looking transitions between light and dark areas.

Let wet tools work for you. Water (for acrylics) or thinner (for oils) in your tool will have more lifting capability if you give it a second or two to react with the paint before you begin lifting the tool. Always quickly blot wet Q-tips on a paper towel before using them—there can be too much of a good thing!

Blending With a Dry Q-tip

Softening an Edge Use dry Q-tips to soften edges. Gently jiggle the Q-tip on the line between the shape and the background to blend, but maintain the initial size of the shape.

Enlarging Shapes To enlarge shapes, place the Q-tip in the white area. Gradually move into the background with a jiggling motion and evenly decreasing pressure.

Reducing Shapes Reduce a shape by moving background paint into it, gradually increasing pressure as you approach the center. The incredible shrinking shape!

Lifting Out With a Wet Brush

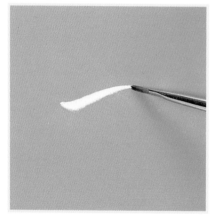

The Wet Brush The wet brush is always a *bright* brush and should have a good chisel edge. To be an effective lift-out tool, it must be used with the *back corner* pressed to the surface and the *top corner* leading the stroke. This position will lift the most paint.

Airplaning Press and jiggle the brush slightly to release some moisture onto the painted surface. Lightly sweep the brush in an airplaning stroke, allowing the brush to swivel some as you move out of the stroke. The top line of your stroke should be cleanly lifted, while the bottom remains hazy.

Scooting the Paint Ahead Use the wet brush with its chisel flat on the surface. A single stroke and no pressure will lift very fine lines. To enlarge shapes, use a zigzag stroke and scoot the paint ahead of the brush.

HOW TO PAINT FUR

Realistic fur can be more fun, faster and easier to paint than you ever thought possible. Just follow the step-by-step paint patterns and then proceed to brush the animal much as you would comb a child's hair or groom your pet. And, as you would with a child or pet, don't stop working until your animal looks perfect!

Use your eyes. If the fur doesn't look right, repeat or alter the process until it does. It's worth the extra trouble because, unlike a child or pet, this little animal is going to stay perfect for longer than ten minutes!

The Paint Pattern

The paint pattern is the foundation for creating realistic fur. It may look like a mess, but in it lies the secret to creating the myriad hues and values we see in real life without having to pre-mix each color—not to mention having to then paint them hair by hair!

Always take a minute to compare the finished paint pattern to the finished painting. This "camouflage paint suit" is easy to decipher if you know what to look for.

First, take note of the dark painted shapes and how they create the deep shadow areas on the finished painting. Next, translate which strokes must be accurately painted to maintain the animal's shape (such as the nose or ear), which strokes are scrumbled in loosely to provide general fur color (as on the hip), and which strokes are really "negative" strokes that define another shape (as on the back). With a little practice, you'll be reading paint patterns easily, and you'll even be able to create your own just by looking at an animal photo.

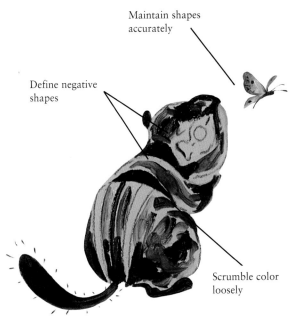

Maintain shapes accurately

Define negative shapes

Scrumble color loosely

How to Build the Paint Pattern

Paint Darks and Shadow Areas Before you begin, paint gel on as much of the animal as you plan to work on at one time. Then paint and shade any major pink areas (such as ears or muzzles). Heavily load a bright brush with your darkest fur color and carefully paint the dark shadow areas. Last, paint any other dark-colored fur areas.

Scrumble in Lighter Color Scrumble lighter color in empty areas. Be sure to leave some background showing. Loose, squiggly shapes of varying depth of paint result in the most realistic-looking fur.

Add Remaining Colors Remaining colors are loosely laid on top of previous colors. Use a heavily loaded brush and let the paint fall off the brush so as not to disturb the colors underneath.

    Check to see if your paint pattern looks like the picture. Make any adjustments needed, and you're ready to almost magically create fur!

Before You Brush Fur . . .

Fur can be tricky. We look at fur all the time, but do we really *see* it? Getting beyond left-brain categories such as "brown/fluffy" or "long/white" is essential—so grab a pet or get a photo and let's study fur!

First, is the fur long or short, sleek or fluffy, coarse or fine, straight or curly? Most fur is straight and doesn't curve much along the length of the hair unless it is very long. Some animals have several lengths of fur. Think of a squirrel's or a fox's tail or the extremely short fur on a Persian cat's face.

About the only thing universal with fur is that it *layers* as it covers the animal's body. Think of it as fringe on a flapper dress—the swinging fringe ends (tips) hanging over the stitched-down top of the fringe (roots).

In this diagram the arrows indicate how most fur actually grows. The tips of the fur layers point away from the nose, going over the head and back, or down the tummy, and out toward the extremities (ears, paws and tail).

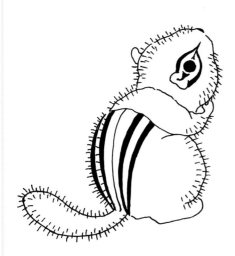

The angle of the layers of hairs to the skin determines how sleek or fluffy the animal is. The smaller the angle, the sleeker the animal, even to the point of looking "greased down."

The greater the angle, the fluffier—or more scared!—the animal appears. Long hair with this angle makes the animal look much larger.

As you layer the rows of fur on your animal, wrap them around and over the curves of the muscles, tips lying over roots of the previous row. Notice that the angles of the hairs in a layer have an orderly sequence as they splay out over the body. This is a vital part of your illusion of roundness.

Perspective changes everything. Sometimes you see less of a hair or only its tip as it points toward your eye, even though you know it is really much longer. Particularly in fluffy fur, perspective will sometimes make the fur appear to be growing in the wrong direction as the fur pops over the curves of the body. Paint what you *see*, not what you *know*!

Brushing Fur With a Bristle Brush

Raking through the paint pattern with a stiff, round bristle brush creates many hair lines at once.

Painted surfaces tend to be slick, so use almost *no pressure* on the brush. Use more pressure on rougher backgrounds. Also, paint will tend to snowplow (pile up) on slick surfaces, so be sure to airplane the brush slightly as you stroke. Clean your brush frequently and moisten it with gel when necessary.

When painting animals on surfaces, the back-and-forth stroke and the strokes using a rake are the most valuable ones in your repertoire. These and the other strokes shown below may be used in any combination. If one isn't working, try another. Experiment! Discover the effects you create with more or less gel, pressure or paint. Now's the time to find out what works best for *you* to create realistic fur.

Back-and-forth strokes quickly and easily produce an area of fur that can then be perfected with other strokes. Remember: no pressure, and airplane the brush.

Dragging out creates nice fur tips. Begin airplaning the brush off the surface in plenty of time, though, or your animal will "keep on growing."

Dragging in with a clean brush thins out heavy fur tips. Airplane into the tips toward the roots, and wipe out the brush after each stroke.

Splatting pushes the paint ahead of the bristles. This stroke quickly creates very tidy, controlled-length edge fur.

Stippling automatically creates fur tips that point directly toward your eye. It is also useful in very tiny areas of short fur, such as paws and small faces.

Extending thin fur, as on tails, is done by dragging a tiny bit of paint out from already-brushed fur tips. Use no overlapping strokes and plenty of gel.

The filbert rake, held with all hairs on the surface and dragged out, makes beautiful fur tips and is essential to good edge fur when working in acrylics. Be sure to airplane the brush!

Let's Practice Brushing

Paint a small tail shape. With back-and-forth or dragging-out strokes, brush the edge fur of the tail. Be mindful of the angle of the hairs as they pop from the skin.

Stipple the center where only the tips of the fur are visible. Check for even rotation of hair angles and lightly re-brush any areas that need further grooming.

Add layers of fur, overlapping each row's tips over the previous row's roots. The rows should wrap around the round tail.

The Rough Brush

The rough (or first) brush should be carefully done but not overworked. Use a light touch and keep overlapping of strokes to a minimum. Clean and re-gel your brush often to prevent colors from traveling or mushing into a single-color animal. Soon, fur will be sprouting out all over your animal, much as grass sprouts on those little ceramic pets!

1 Study this fur diagram. Mentally picture how short or long, sleek or fluffy, you want your chipmunk's fur to be.

2 Begin by brushing the fur on the edges of the animal with a bristle brush or a rake. Pay particular attention to the length and angle of the hairs.

Rough Brush (Continued)

3 Next, with a bristle brush, brush the underneath layers of fur. Layer tips over roots, brushing the top layers of fur last.

4 Stipple the areas closest to the eye, where only the tips of the hairs are visible as they point toward your eye.

5 Adjust the color levels of your fur by directly adding more or other colors where needed. Now, your animal is still a bit scruffy, but you're seeing the possibilities of a little tender loving care!

Glow and Re-Brush

"Glowing" simulates the reflection of light off the fur. Think of glows as sunbeams bouncing off the rounded parts of the body closest to your eye. The results will be fantastic three-dimensional, realistic fur! This is also the final grooming stage of brushing fur. As you glow, inspect your animal's fur for any other places that could use your attention.

BEFORE YOU GLOW . . .
Compare the glow pattern (below right) to the finished painting (below left). Notice the relative size of the lifted-out glow areas to the finished glow. Plan to do the large, easy Q-tip glows first, saving the smaller glows for last.

Dry-Glowing Techniques

Always begin glowing with this technique. Frequently, dry-glowing produces sufficient glowing when painting animals on painted and other slick surfaces—especially with oil paint. Acrylic paint may need more wet-glowing to remain workable.

1 Lift the glow area with a clean, dry Q-tip. The area should be larger than the final glow. Use more pressure for brighter glows, less for softer glows (or where the fur simply needs to be a lighter color).

2 Begin re-brushing the glow area on the outer edge. Wipe out and re-gel your brush often to achieve a smooth transition from the dark edge to the light center. Repeat as necessary until your glow is the correct shape, size and intensity.

Wet-Brush Glowing Techniques

Wet-brush glowing is used for bright highlights in tiny spaces.

Use a bright brush that has been dipped in water (for acrylics) or thinner (for oils) and squeezed or wiped out. Stroke on the back corner of the chisel for a clean lift-out, then very carefully re-brush with a small bristle brush. If your glow disappears in the re-brush, just glow and re-brush again. These little ones can be a real vanishing act!

Wet Q-tip Glowing Techniques

Wet Q-tip glowing can be used alone or to brighten centers of areas already dry Q-tip-glowed. Lift out only one or two wet glows at a time, as the moisture (be it water for acrylics or thinner for oils) must not evaporate before the glow is re-brushed.

Lift paint from the area to be glowed by slightly jiggling the wet Q-tip to release a bit of liquid onto the surface. Enlarge the shape, using no pressure. The shape should be larger than the final highlight and have a "soupy-painty" ring around it.

Re-brush the glow, moving from its edge to the center. For brilliant glows, avoid letting the brush touch the white pinpoint center. Wipe out and re-gel your brush often, as the gel will retain individual hair marks when you move through the "soupy-painty" ring. The re-gelled brush also increasingly transparentizes the paint as you approach the center of the glow. Repeat as needed when glows seem to vanish or take on strange shapes.

Some designs call for white paint added into a few previously glowed areas. Use a rake reloaded with clean paint after each individual stroke for sparkling white fur tips. Once you're satisfied with the tips, gently blend in the white roots with a bristle brush.

Now that your fur is brushed and glowed, you're ready to add any fur markings such as stripes or spots. When working on very small animals, it is sometimes easier to perfect your work with a wet-brush lift-out than to paint or brush it perfectly in the beginning. Your wet-brush "eraser" insures no-fail painting!

FINISHING TRICKS

Sharp edges, such as eyes and ribbons have, are created by first painting the middle of the shape and then stretching the paint almost to the edges. Finish by stretching the existing paint to the final edge with a clean, wet brush.

Round, hard shapes, such as eyes, are best done with loose paint. Let the paint flow off a heavily loaded brush and then move the paint in an ever-larger circle, with the hairs of the brush touching only the paint, not the surface. "Stirring your puddle" this way allows the paint to form its own perfect edge!

Pinpoint highlights are easy if you heavily load the brush with loose paint and let the paint flow off the brush. Since the hairs of the brush never touch the underlying paint, a sparkling round highlight will float on the surface.

Pinpoint darks blended into the very deepest shadows help define the animal's shape. Go easy, as just a touch of paint goes a long way. It may be safer to do this when the fur is dry. Just paint the pinpoint and then blend it into the fur with gel.

Less is best. Removing paint altogether or manipulating existing paint with a clean, wet brush results in very delicate effects. Experiment with putting on less and taking off more!

And Finally . . .

- *Drying times* can be manipulated. *Oil color's* drying can be accelerated by adding chemical driers. They are not recommended for most fur painting in this technique, but they work well in slow-drying finish-work colors. Follow manufacturer's directions carefully. *Acrylic color's* drying can be retarded with extenders for finish work. For fur, in this technique, the extenders thin the paint too much. Instead, add a few drops of glycerin emollient to your blending gel and keep ice in your water and under your palette.

- *Practice* before you begin a project using this unusual technique. Paint just parts of animals, such as tails, ears or hips, to acquaint yourself with the method. A piece of either Masonite or heavy cold-press illustration board, basecoated and then sprayed with Krylon #1311 Matte Finishing Spray, is a good practice surface.

1
Joy to the World!

I'm a bit shy about giving my work as gifts. Will the recipient want to hang

the painting, I wonder, or use the decorated tray? Will the gift be treasured?

But holiday ornaments free me of these worries. Everyone enjoys them.

Painting these little birdlets on a Christmas ball is a fun project

that will always end up on the front of the tree!

Preparing Your Ornament

Wipe your ornament clean with a vinegar solution using a soft paper towel. Frosted ornaments scratch easily, so work with care on this project.

What You'll Need

- 3¼″ frosted ornament from Cabin Crafters
- Glass preparation and finishing materials
- Pen
- Soft lead pencil
- Mechanical pencil or stylus
- Tracing paper
- Scotch Magic Tape
- Used packing-tape ring
- Angled brush and white acrylic paint for undercoat
- Synthetic steel wool or brown paper bag
- Q-tips and soft paper towels
- Gold fine-point Pilot pen
- Brushes—tiny round hair, small bright hair, medium bright hair, small bristle round, medium bristle round, small filbert rake, small mop (optional)

OIL SUPPLIES
Gel medium, odorless thinner, Copal painting medium (optional, for holly), white, Ivory Black, Raw Umber, Cadmium Yellow Light, Burnt Sienna, Sap Green, Vermilion Permanent. Mix these colors: pink, black-basic green, yellow-basic green.

ACRYLIC SUPPLIES
Gel medium, water, floating medium (optional), gloss water-based varnish to mix into colors (or use water-based enamel paints), white, Pure Black, Raw Umber, Medium Yellow, Burnt Sienna, Sap Green, Red Light. Mix these colors: pink, black-basic green, yellow-basic green.

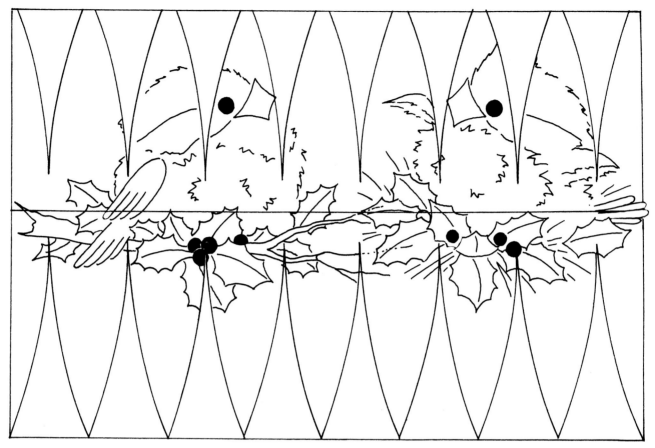

This pattern may be hand-traced or photocopied for personal use only. Enlarge at 105% to bring it up to full size.

Before You Paint

1 Trace with a pen and then cut out the "orange-peel" pattern. On the back of your tracing, retrace the pattern with a soft lead pencil. Attach a small piece of tape to each orange-peel point. Remove the gold hanger and then tape the orange-peel sections to the ball, taping the central section first and keeping the "equator" level as it encircles the ball.

2 Prop the ball in a tape ring. Hold the ball by inserting a finger in the hole and retrace the pattern on the ball using a mechanical pencil or stylus.

3 The orange-peel pattern facilitates an accurate, undistorted transfer to the curved surface of the ball.

Undercoat the Design

4 Paint the undercoat with a filbert rake and white acrylic paint, leaving the interior lines of the pattern visible. Feather the exterior edges of the birdlet in the direction the feathers grow.

5 Smooth the dry paint with a synthetic steel wool pad or a piece of brown paper bag.

Pre-Mix Your Paint

Because varnishing will remove the frosting from the ball, pre-mix your paint with a medium that won't dilute it too much but will allow the design to have some sheen when dry. Res-n-gel Non-Toxic, some drying oils or Copal varnish work in oil. With acrylic, mix some gloss water-based varnish into your color or experiment with one of the new water-based enamels.

Paint the Eye

6 Stir a small puddle of black paint with a tiny round brush until it enlarges to the correct size and shape of the eye.

7 Correct any imperfections by cleaning up the edge with a clean, wet, small bright brush. A perfect white ring should be left around the black eye.

Gel and Paint Bright Red Feathers

8 *Always cover the undercoat with gel* in the area you plan to work. Depending on your medium, this may be a very small area or the entire birdlet.

Paint a base of bright red using a filbert rake and thick paint. Leave unpainted some areas that will be black or shadowed (such as close to the eye and under the beak). Establish fairly finished edge feathers as you work.

Paint Highlights and Shadows

9 Heavily load a medium bright brush with yellow and paint loose yellow highlight areas. Let the paint fall off the brush, stirring up the underlying red as little as possible.

10 Wipe out your yellow brush, reload with Burnt Sienna and paint shadow areas in the feathers.

11 Paint the deepest shadow areas with black, being sure to leave a pretty beak shape. Don't worry that your birdlet now looks like a gloppy, gooey mess—he's just right!

The Feather Pattern

12 Take a minute to relate this feather diagram to the finished birdlet at right. Notice the direction and angles of the feathers as they go from the beak back over the head and out the wings. The breast feathers are depicted as a puff-ball to make the birdlet look cute and fluffy.

Rough-Brush the Feathers

13 Brush the edge feathers of each shape by dragging a small amount of paint into the background with a clean filbert rake or bristle brush. Wipe the brush clean and moisten with gel as needed to produce good tips. Proceed to layer the feathers, tips over roots, with a bristle brush. Brush through the deep paint with a "tickle touch," wiping and re-gelling the brush as necessary to prevent excess traveling of color.

Add Black Markings

14 (Left) With a tiny round brush, paint the black mask. Start away from the white eye ring, gradually sneaking up to the ring and scooting the paint ahead of the brush. Remember, if you make a mess, clean it up with a wet-brush "eraser."

15 (Right) Add wing markings with a tiny round brush. Your birdlet is now obviously a redbird, but he lacks luster and life.

Lift Out and Add White to Some Glow Areas

16 (Left) With a wet Q-tip, gently remove paint from areas to be highlighted. Be careful to avoid drips or runs from the Q-tip caused by the curved surface of the ball.

17 (Right) Add thick white paint to the lifted-out areas with a medium bright brush. Heavily load the brush so the paint will fall off the brush and won't pick up red.

Re-Brush and Groom

18 After moistening your clean bristle brush with gel, re-brush the glowed white areas. An extremely light touch and frequent cleaning and re-gelling are essential, especially as you approach areas that must remain bright white.

19 You may have to glow, paint white and re-brush an area more than once to achieve the effect you want. Try using a filbert rake and a feather touch on the brightest feathers. Clean and reload the filbert after every stroke, or you'll have a pink bird—not a red one!

20 Once you're satisfied with your birdlet's feathers, load a tiny round brush with loose paint and float a white droplet on the eye for a highlight. Your finished birdlet is almost ready to burst into song.

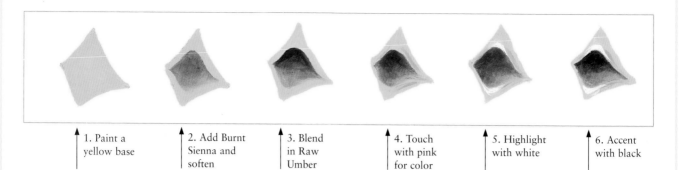

↑ 1. Paint a yellow base

↑ 2. Add Burnt Sienna and soften

↑ 3. Blend in Raw Umber

↑ 4. Touch with pink for color

↑ 5. Highlight with white

↑ 6. Accent with black

The Beak

This is the basic sequence for painting the beak with a small bright and a tiny round brush. If you are working in oil, begin with a sheer but sticky yellow beak. Wipe the brush clean (no thinner) and reload with Burnt Sienna. Again, wipe the brush clean (no thinner) and blend the colors. Repeat for Raw Umber. Finish with very loose pink, white and black. If you are painting with acrylics, use the blending or floating techniques you prefer.

Paint the Greenery

21 (Top) Using two or three shades of basic green (add black or yellow to vary), paint and blend the holly leaves. Always begin painting in the center of the leaf, allowing the paint to become more sheer at the edges. For even crisper, sharper-looking leaves, clean the edges with your wet brush "eraser." Use a tiny mop brush to blend areas. Veins can be either lifted out or painted on with a tiny round brush. Several coats may be necessary to make the leaves opaque. Avoid muddy colors by allowing the leaves to dry before painting the berries.

22 (Middle) Stir a small puddle of red paint with a tiny round brush until you've enlarged it to the right size and shape for a holly berry. Stir a bit of yellow into the middle of the berry until it blends. Heavily load your smallest round brush and let a droplet of white fall off the brush to create a sparkling highlight.

23 Begin freehanding dark green needles with very thin paint and a tiny round brush. Always airplane your strokes for beautiful tapered needles. Use these needles to block in the general shape of a clump of needles. Be careful to watch the composition you are creating. Add varying shades of basic green needles as you work.

Once several layers of needles have been painted, you can create interesting color variations by stroking with a brush loaded with only yellow, or with no paint at all—instant shading!

Finishing Your Ornament

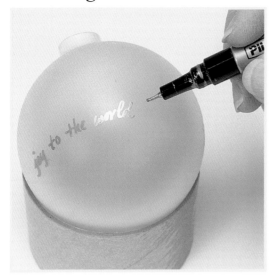

24 Write the title, date or special holiday greeting on the back of the ball with a gold Pilot pen.

25 Let it snow! Vary the size and spacing of your flakes to create a natural look. Try gently pressing your finger on a white dot to create large, fluffy flakes. If you are working in oil, paint flakes on the design in oil, but use acrylic on the rest of the ball for easier handling.

Copal Painting Medium

Mixed with oil paints, Copal Painting Medium produces rich jewel-tone colors on glass. Always follow the label precautions. Let the Copal-paint mixture stand uncovered for about an hour before painting in order to thicken the mixture. This makes beautiful shiny leaves such as holly and magnolia.

26 Tie on a bow and you've created a keepsake ornament to be handed down over many Christmases to come. Maybe, like me, you'll be inspired to paint a different birdlet each year—a chickadee, a bluebird, a hummingbird. Give yourself plenty of lead time, though, because it seems everybody wants one!

2

Hickory Dickory Dock

Children love mice! They're enchanted by stories such as *Cinderella*,

The Tailor of Gloucester, *The Mouse and the Motorcycle*, and

If You Give a Mouse a Cookie. I still love these stories, and

painting these wee creatures makes me feel young at heart.

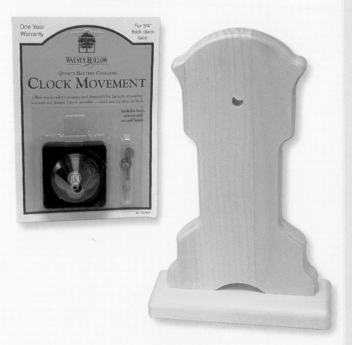

What You'll Need

- 9½" wood clock and clockworks from Walnut Hollow
- Set of tiny clock hands (1" or less) from Walnut Hollow
- Self-adhesive face numerals (optional)
- Wood preparation and finishing materials
- Base-coating materials—cream color acrylic paint for base coat, Warm White acrylic paint for clock face
- Heavy coated paper or stencil blank for the clock face stencil
- Krylon #1311 Matte Finishing Spray
- Mechanical pencil
- Tracing paper
- Grey transfer paper
- Scotch Magic Tape
- White acrylic paint for undercoat
- Piece of brown paper bag
- Q-tips and soft paper towels
- Gold fine-point pen or paint
- Brushes—tiny round hair, small bright hair, medium bright hair, small bristle round, small filbert rake, small mop (optional)

OIL SUPPLIES
Gel medium, odorless thinner, white, Ivory Black, Raw Umber, Cadmium Yellow Light, Burnt Sienna, Vermilion Permanent. Mix these colors: pink, soft brown, fawn.

ACRYLIC SUPPLIES
Gel medium, water, floating medium (optional), white, Pure Black, Raw Umber, Medium Yellow, Burnt Sienna, True Burgundy, Hauser Green Dark. Mix these colors: pink, soft brown, fawn.

Preparing Your Surface

This design is adaptable to many styles and sizes of clocks. But keep in mind that these very tiny mice will be difficult to paint much smaller and will lose their cuteness if you paint them much larger. Gesso your prepared surface when painting very small animals. Base-coat the clock in a cream color, water-based paint and mist with Krylon #1311 Matte Finishing Spray. You may wish to use adhesive numerals to save yourself some work.

Before You Paint Fur

This pattern may be hand-traced or photocopied for personal use only. Enlarge at 119% to bring it up to full size.

Note

You may choose to paint the clock pendulum and moldings before the mice are painted.

1 Cut a stencil for the clock face. Load a large brush with Warm White acrylic paint and paint the clock face using the stencil. Begin each stroke outside the rim on the stencil and drag the brush toward the center of the face. This prevents paint from building up around the edges or bleeding under the stencil.

2 Transfer your pattern using grey transfer paper. These are very delicate animals, so trace with a mechanical pencil and wipe the back of the transfer paper with a soft paper towel to insure pale, thin transfer lines. Undercoat future white areas and glow areas of the mice with white acrylic paint, leaving no ridges. (You may wish to paint a thin coat of white paint over each entire mouse if your surface became too slick with Krylon.) Smooth the undercoat with a brown paper bag.

3 Paint gel and then pink on the ears and muzzles of the mice with a small bright brush. Lift out and then blend the pink with a wet or dry Q-tip to create exquisite "seashell" ears. Blend in some white paint if needed.

Paint Shadows and Add Color

4 (Left) *First, paint gel over all areas you are working on.* Paint the deep shadows and darker areas with soft brown, using an amply loaded small bright brush. As your brush unloads, paint the sketchy, lighter brown areas. Less paint in the gel automatically creates a more transparent, lighter brown. Use loose squiggly strokes. Remember that these are itty-bitty creatures, so paint their dainty bodies precisely. Be particularly careful where a stroke defines another shape (such as an ear).

5 (Right) With loose strokes and a lightly loaded small bright brush, fill in blank areas with fawn. The fawn strokes should have a semitransparent look and some base coat should still show. You can always add more color later if you need it.

Rough-Brush the Fur

6 Compare this fur diagram to the finished painting on page 43 and to the rough brush in the next photo. Analyze how the fur grows away from the nose, over the body, and out to the paws and end of the tail. Notice that only the tips of the hairs show on the hip and shoulder as you look straight down the hair shafts. Take a minute to consider how short each hair stroke must be on these tiny creatures—we don't want angora guinea pigs.

7 Soften the brown ear canals with a tightly wound, dry Q-tip, leaving the side closest to the forehead darker. With a small bristle brush, a feather touch and extremely short back-and-forth strokes, begin to brush the fur. Create perfect edge fur using a filbert rake. Interior fur needn't be quite so groomed, but you will need to wipe and re-gel your bristle brush frequently to prevent the dark shadows from traveling. Keep the cheek of the lower mouse light, so the tiny paw will show up later.

Check the color intensity of your mice with the mice in the photo above. If your color is weak, brush in more color with a bristle brush.

Glow Some Areas

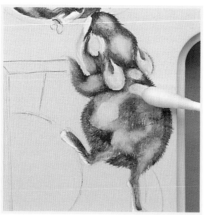

8 Study the finished mice on page 43 to determine which areas of your mice need to be glowed. Begin with a dry Q-tip in large, obvious areas first. This will not only simplify the process, but will also make you feel as if you're really making rapid progress.

9 Some very bright highlights will require a wet Q-tip glow in the dry glow area. Just a few will do for now, as we don't want a "Swiss cheese" mouse. You can always add more later. Wet Q-tip glows must be re-brushed immediately, so work them one or two at a time.

10 Tiny glows are best lifted out with a wet or dry small bright brush. Just like larger glows, these lift-outs should begin larger than the finished glowed area. If too small, they will totally disappear in the re-brush!

Re-Brush and Groom

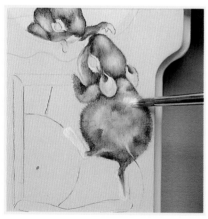

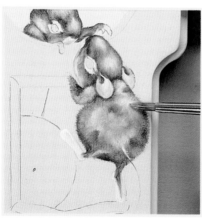

11 With a clean bristle brush moistened in gel, re-brush glowed areas. Wipe clean and re-gel the brush constantly as you brush toward the middle of a glowed area. The result: automatic shading!

For soft, hazy highlights, let some transparent color travel into the center. For brightest highlights, never allow the brush to touch the center of a glowed area. A touch of white paint blended into these glows produces a downy effect.

12 Soft pink blended into a few of the glowed areas furthers the illusion of a baby animal.

13 Brush in some Burnt Sienna mixed with gel to bring warmth and life to the fur. Now is the time to look at your baby animal and ask, "Are you groomed?" Find one tiny adjustment to make and do it. Then look for another. You'll be amazed at how a series of minor corrections will improve your baby animal—and you thought you were done!

Finishing Your Mice

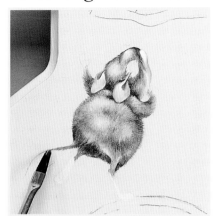

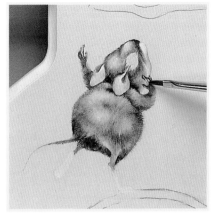

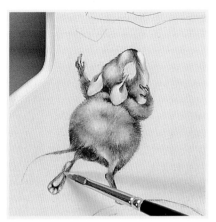

14 Carefully paint the tails using soft brown mixed with some gel and a filbert rake. Keep the hair smooth on the top of the tails and raked at a slight angle on the underside for the best effect.

15 Believe it or not, the best brush for creating tiny "hands" is a small bright. Use lightly gelled brown paint to stroke the "fingers." Wipe the brush clean and lift out some highlights. Then, with a clean wet brush, clean up and reshape individual parts. On tiny animals, this is easier than painting precisely to begin with.

16 Create pads and toes on the feet by lifting out the shapes with a small, wet bright brush. Paint in pink and shade with white. Slim the fragile ankles with a wet brush if they grew thick in brushing.

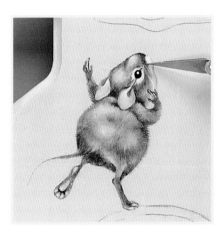

17 Stir small puddles of black paint until they are the correct size to make bright, beady eyes for your mice. Float a tiny droplet of white for sparkle. Let the white fall off the brush without allowing the brush hairs to touch the black paint. This will form instant, perfect round highlights. Add twitchy whiskers with an X-Acto knife, and your mouse is a small bundle of personality!

Painting the Pendulum

Paint Raw Umber and fawn on a gel undercoat

Paint the hanger

Drag through paint with a filbert rake

Float more bright whites with filbert rake

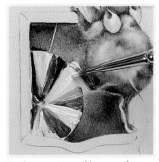

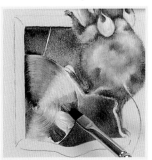

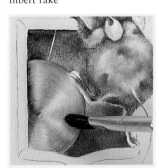

Stipple-blend with a bristle brush

Radiate stripes of brown, fawn, yellow and white from center

If needed, add some Burnt Sienna and re-rake

Soften with a mop for a shimmering effect

Finishing Your Clock

Try these simple techniques to faux-finish the base, pendulum case and face moldings of your clock.

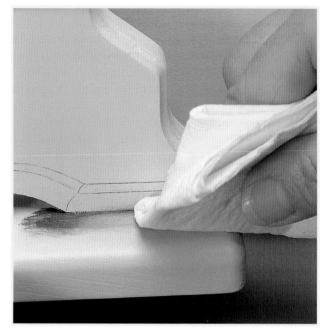

18 Paint a mixture of soft brown and gel over the base area to be antiqued. Wipe off and blend with a soft paper towel.

19 Roughly paint molding lines with soft brown. Then, smudge and blend with a dry Q-tip.

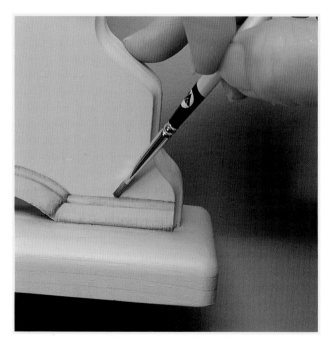

20 Clean up and sharpen edges with a wet medium bright brush.

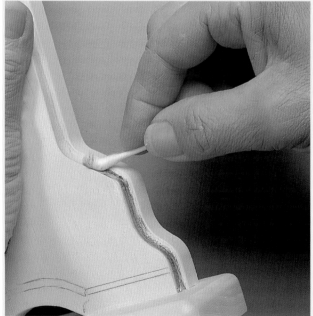

21 For an even greater dimensional effect, paint edge grooves with a mixture of soft brown and gel and soften with a dry Q-tip.

Final Touches

First, test your gold pen or gold paint to make sure it is smudge-proof when varnished. Then, following either a paper template or erasable guidelines, write (or paint) the gold nursery rhyme. Most gold inks can be removed with odorless thinner if you make a mistake. Plan ahead, practice, and execute your lettering with great care. It is every bit as important as your mice and can make or break your project. You may prefer to skip the rhyme and use only *Hickory Dickory Dock* on the base.

Paint or adhere numerals to the face. I chose to use the traditional clock Roman numeral for four—IIII—because it balances better compositionally with VIII.

Varnish your clock with several coats of water-based satin varnish. **Caution:** Do not sand between the first and second coats of varnish, because you could damage the delicate raised fur lines. For added beauty, wax your clock.

Install the clockworks, using hands that are sized correctly for the face. All that's left is to wait and see if your mice run when the clock strikes one!

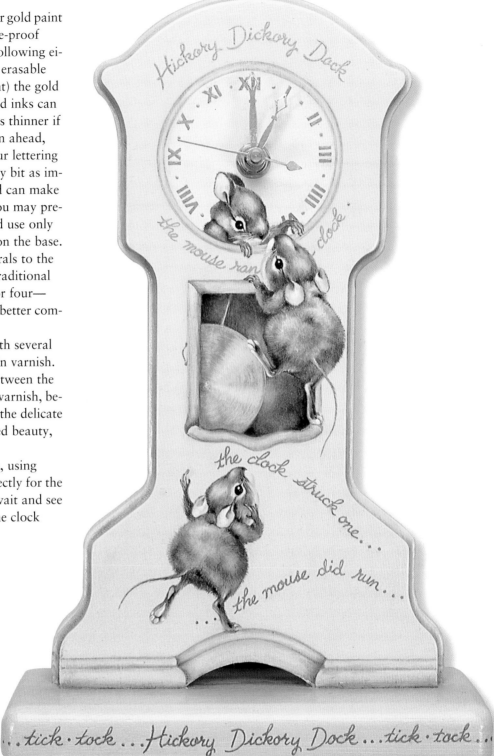

3

Hush Puppy

I can't resist trusting eyes, whether they belong to small

children or pets. Just one of "those looks" at the end of the day, and

you forget all about the muddy clothes or the chewed-up shoe.

"Hush little baby, all's safe with the world, lights out, sleep tight."

What You'll Need

- 4″-diameter punched tin box and wooden lid from Cabin Craft
- Three wood balls for feet from Cabin Craft
- Wood glue
- Sound reflector and music box (Brahms' Lullabye) from Cabin Craft
- OR: Switch plate from Cabin Craft
- Pushpin
- Tin and wood preparation and finishing materials
- Base-coating materials
- Light blue-grey acrylic paint for base coat
- Angled brush and Wicker White acrylic paint for undercoat and bedding
- Krylon #1311 Matte Finishing Spray
- Mechanical pencil or stylus
- Tracing paper
- Transfer paper—white and grey
- X-Acto knife
- Scotch Magic Tape
- Piece of heavy brown paper bag
- Q-tips and soft paper towels
- Lift-out tool (optional)
- Brushes—tiny round hair, small bright hair, medium bright hair, small bristle round, medium bristle round, small filbert rake, small mop

OIL SUPPLIES
Gel medium, odorless thinner, white, Ivory Black, Raw Umber, Cadmium Yellow Light, Burnt Sienna, Vermilion Permanent, Prussian Blue. Mix these colors: pink, soft brown, basic blue-grey, basic green.

ACRYLIC SUPPLIES
Gel medium, water, floating medium (optional), Wicker White, Pure Black, Raw Umber, Medium Yellow, Burnt Sienna, True Burgundy, Hauser Green Dark, Red Light, Prussian Blue. Mix these colors: pink, soft brown, basic blue-grey, basic green.

Preparing Your Surface

Drill or punch a hole in the bottom of the tin box for the music box key. Prepare the tin and wood and then base-coat with light blue-grey. Allow the top middle hole of each punched heart to fill with paint. Keep the other holes open by punching them with a pushpin.

Stick the wooden ball feet to your work surface with Scotch Magic Tape to hold them in place while you paint and dry them. Then there is only a small spot left to cover.

Mist all surfaces with Krylon #1311 Matte Finishing Spray to keep them impervious to dirt and stray paint smudges. (Note: You may wish to transfer the tin design with white transfer paper before you spray, so it won't rub off as you paint later.)

These patterns may be hand-traced or photocopied for personal use only. Enlarge at 125% to bring them up to full size.

Before You Paint

1 Trace the pattern and then transfer the design outline with white transfer paper. Undercoat the puppy, sheet and pillow ruffle with white acrylic paint. Use an angular brush to feather the fur edges as you work.

Paint the ruffle and sheet with Wicker White, fading the sheet into the blue-grey as it nears the lid edges. Use your choice of blending or floating techniques.

2 Smooth the paint with a piece of brown paper bag. Transfer the interior design with grey transfer paper. Paint the quilt lines with watery white acrylic to preserve them for painting later, or shade the quilt now. Use acrylic paint and your choice of blending or floating techniques.

Gel and then paint the heart pillow using basic blue-grey (or darker). If you are working in oil, blend thick paint with a mop brush and a feather touch. In acrylic, use whichever floating or blending methods work best for you.

Start in the Middle

3 Paint the paw pads pink so they won't get lost in all this fur. (We'll shade them later.) Begin your pup by painting a thick dab of soft brown in the middle of each eye and the nose.

If you are working in acrylic, brush the eye areas with gel before painting, and don't paint the nose at all yet. If you are working in oil, gel isn't necessary under small eyes.

With a small bright brush, push the existing paint just short of the eyeball shape. Using a clean tiny round brush and no more paint, continue to push the paint to form the sphere. Paint that is more sheer at the very edge of a shape makes for precise, crisp edges. If you make a mess, lift the mistake with a wet bright brush and try again. Eyes are too important to leave less than perfect!

Glow the eyes with a dry Q-tip and paint the mouth black. Outline the eyes in black with a tiny round brush. Again, start away from the rim, *sneak up* gradually and correct if you slip.

Paint the Shadows and Darks

4 *First, paint gel over all areas you are working.* Then heavily load a medium bright brush with black and paint the deep shadow areas first. As the brush unloads, move to the more transparent black strokes. Don't worry about painting an exact copy of the photo. We have many more steps, so for now just paint loose strokes somewhat in the direction the fur grows. Be sure to hold the major shapes, such as the ears and muzzle, and keep the darkest shadows dark.

5 Paint soft brown in some areas for color variation in the fur. Let it be somewhat transparent. Fill in remaining blank areas with rather gloppy white. Oh my—what a mess!

Rough-Brush the Fur

6 Compare this fur diagram to the finished painting on page 51 and to the rough-brush photo at the right. Think about how long the fur is (it varies from muzzle to ear), where it is straight or curved, or short, or fluffy. Observe areas that should not be overworked now, since they will be extensively glowed and reworked later.

7 A very light touch is essential for creating long, silky fur. Clean and moisten your bristle brush with gel often to create the maximum number of hues and values of color. Try to maintain important shapes and light and dark areas as you stroke. Where color looks weak, add more with the bristle brush. Use a filbert rake to extend the long edge fur, grabbing paint from just the tips of what you brushed previously. This will cure your puppy's split ends, but she still needs a good conditioner!

Glow and Re-Brush the Fur

8 Constantly compare your puppy to the photos above and at the right as you glow and re-brush. Long, tangled fur can seem overwhelming at first, so it's best to concentrate on one shape (or even part of a shape) at a time.

Begin by glowing large, obvious shapes with a dry Q-tip and re-brushing the shape with a bristle brush. Re-glow with a wet Q-tip where needed. Once your major shapes have been established, move on to smaller shapes and wet-brush glowing.

9 Re-brush glows with either a bristle brush or a filbert rake. Keep fiddling and futzing, re-glowing and re-brushing, adding and removing paint in *one* major shape (ears, forehead, muzzle, paws) at a time. Believe me, you *will* discover order in this chaos! Your puppy's watching you, so be as patient as she is.

Grooming Your Puppy

10 With a wet medium bright brush, lift out some individual shining hairs. This is fun to do, so exercise a bit of control or you'll create a bedraggled, wet pup.

11 Soften the fur with a dry mop and a tickle touch. Now *this* is the fur you've been waiting for!

12 Very fine hairs are easily created with an X-Acto knife. Again, go easy. Avoid a "pincushion" pup. Remember, we're creating the *illusion* of hair-by-hair painting—not really doing it!

Finishing Your Puppy

13 (Left) Finish the tongue and paw pads with more pink, and shade them with white. Brush a few hairs over the pads.

14 (Right) Clean the sheet of any paint smudges with a lift-out brush.

Paint and blend shadows in the sheet under each paw so the pup looks nestled in.

Painting the Eyes and Nose

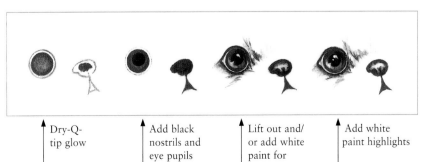

Paint brown in the middle

Stretch the paint to the edge

Dry-Q-tip glow

Add black nostrils and eye pupils

Lift out and/ or add white paint for shading

Add white paint highlights

Final Details

15 Blend, double-load or float these colors to create a shining ribbon. Sharpen edges with a wet-brush cleanup if needed.

↑ Yellow   ↑ Fawn and Burnt Sienna   ↑ White   ↑ Finished ribbon

16 Paint and shade the ruffles with thin blue-grey paint. Shading is simple with dry Q-tips. Clean up and sharpen the edges of the ruffle with a wet lift-out brush.

The eyelet edging is easy when done with a dot of paint on the point of a lift-out tool. Press lightly and watch embroidered holes appear! Accent your ruffles with dark blue-grey.

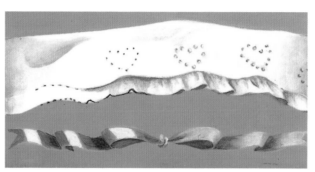

17 Blend, double-load or float white and blue-grey to create the ribbon borders on the box.

Create three-dimensional rosebuds with very thick paint and a tiny round brush. Use shades of pink and yellow double-loaded with white. Add green leaf tips peeking out.

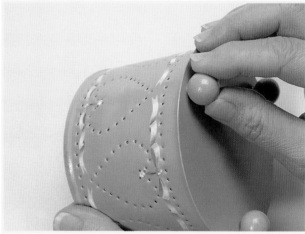

18 Glue three ball feet onto the bottom of the box.

Detail the Quilt, and Finish

19 Gel, paint and shade the quilt. A small mop is especially useful for oil paint. Paint the dotted Swiss using a brush or the point of a lift-out tool. Then, "embroider" the white bow on the pillow. Add raised rosebuds to the quilt and pillow.

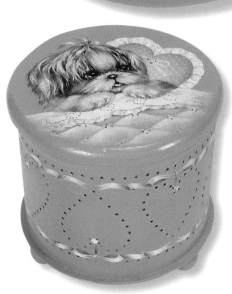

20 Apply several coats of water-based satin varnish. **Caution:** Do not sand between the first and second coats of varnish; you could damage the delicate raised fur lines. Wax the box, including the underside of the lid. This prevents the lid sticking to the base, especially if you live in a warm climate.

Finish your project by installing a tinkling music box. After all, this little puppy needs a lullabye!

Hush Puppy Light Switch Paint the basic design, following the music box directions but reversing the colors on the quilt.

Paint the teddy bear much as you would a mouse or bunny. Be sure to varnish the painted switch "arm" heavily, since he'll be waving "nite-nite" for many bedtimes to come.

4
Outfoxed!

For many years, we were blessed with a red fox family living

just up the hill from our home. They drank from the stream, preened on the

rock wall, and paraded the kits along the garden fence. What artist

can resist painting these gorgeous creatures? I can't.

Preparing Your Surface

Slate is for you if you haven't the patience for prepping wood! Also, paint glides on slate (even over the bumps) and lifts off smooth as butter for corrections.

Clean the slate with soap and water or a vinegar solution. You may wish to seal the surface with wood sealer, if you paint with acrylics, to prevent the slate from absorbing the paint.

What You'll Need

- 10″×7″ tombstone slate from Cape Cod Cooperage
- OR: 5″ oval slates from Cape Cod Cooperage
- Silk rope and tassels (optional)
- Slate preparation and finishing materials
- Angled brush and white acrylic paint for undercoating
- Mechanical pencil or stylus
- Tracing paper
- Transfer paper—grey and white
- X-Acto knife
- Scotch Magic Tape
- Synthetic steel wool pad (#0000) or pieces of brown paper bag
- Q-tips and soft paper towels
- Brushes—tiny round hair, small bright hair, medium bright hair, small bristle round, medium bristle round, small filbert rake, small mop

OIL SUPPLIES

Gel medium, odorless thinner, white, Ivory Black, Raw Umber, Cadmium Yellow Light, Burnt Sienna, Sap Green, Vermilion Permanent. Mix these colors: fawn, basic green.

ACRYLIC SUPPLIES

Gel medium, water, floating medium (optional), white, Pure Black, Raw Umber, Medium Yellow, Burnt Sienna, True Burgundy, Hauser Green Dark, Sap Green, Red Light. Mix these colors: fawn, basic green.

This pattern may be hand-traced or photo-copied for personal use only. The pattern is shown full size.

Before You Paint

1 Trace the pattern and then transfer the design outline with white transfer paper. Undercoat the area with white acrylic paint, feathering fur edges as you paint. Begin with a thin coat. Several coats will be necessary on this dark surface. Make the paint totally opaque on future white fur and glow areas.

Apply paint thickly over ridge areas, then sand to level the surface. Smooth the surface with a synthetic steel wool pad or piece of brown paper bag.

2 Transfer the interior design using grey transfer paper. Refine the edge-fur feathering with a filbert rake. *Paint a layer of gel* over any area you plan to work on. Paint the white muzzle fur.

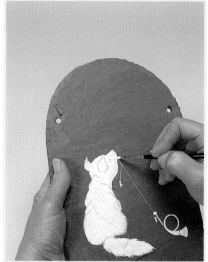

Note

The photos show the tail being worked in each step. It is probably best, however, to paint the tail after the rest of the fox is finished to avoid smearing the paint with your hand.

Paint the Shadows and Add Color

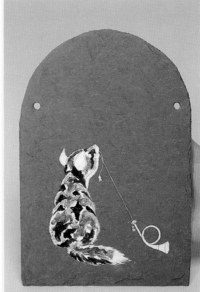

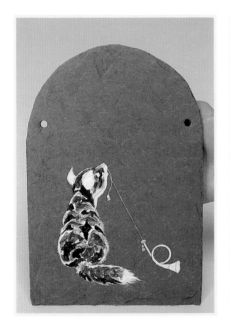

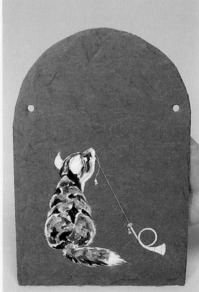

3 (Left) First, paint Raw Umber shadows over the gel. Use a medium bright brush and a heavy load of paint for deep shadows. Paint accurately the shadows that are defining other shapes, such as shoulders and hips. As the brush unloads, paint other brown fur areas. Paint with smooth flowing strokes. Let the brush do the work!

4 (Right) With large squiggly strokes, scrumble in fawn. It should look somewhat transparent but not weak. This is the color that controls the reds and yellows and keeps them from becoming violent. Some of the white undercoat should still show.

5 (Left) Look at the rough-brush photo on page 56. In areas where the fox's color will be reddest, layer some thick Burnt Sienna over the fawn and Raw Umber. Try not to disturb the underlying color. As the brush unloads, scrumble Burnt Sienna in less reddish areas.

6 (Right) Thin your yellow paint to soupy but not runny consistency. Heavily load your medium bright brush. Let the paint fall off the brush so that it will float atop the other colors. Yellow is responsible for vibrant highlights in red fur, so it should be heaviest on areas that will be glowed.

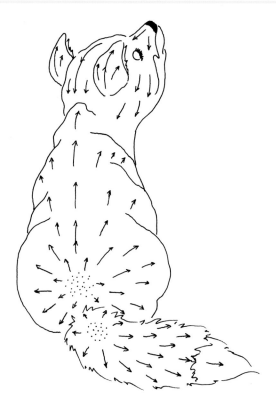

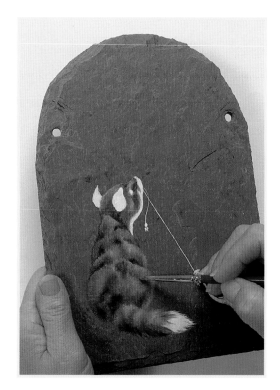

Rough-Brush the Fur

7 As you compare the fur pattern to the finished fox on page 59 and the rough-brush photo above, observe the three different lengths of fur: short on the face and head, medium on the body and long on the tail.

Fur tips actually point away from the nose toward the paws and tail, but study how fluffy fur in perspective often seems to point in the wrong direction. This is because fluffy fur is almost perpendicular to the skin. As the skin molds to the underlying muscles, the fur pops up over the body curves, and we look down the hair shafts. It all depends on the vantage point.

8 (Top right) If your confidence is sagging as you look at the multicolored mess you've created, ignore it and just forge on! You're on your way to gorgeous red fur in no time. Here are some tips to help:

- Brush fur edges with a back-and-forth stroke, a bristle brush and no pressure.
- Extend beautiful edge-fur tips with a filbert rake.
- Use gel sparingly in deep paint.
- As you layer fur around the fox, paint many layers for a bushy look.
- Brush from Burnt Sienna/yellow areas into Raw Umber so the fox stays red, not brown.
- *Wipe your brush often* for less color traveling. The object is to blend, not destroy, the myriad hues.
- When brushing the tail, start short and extend the fur cautiously; tails "grow" before you know it.
- Airplane, airplane, airplane your strokes!

Glow Some Areas

9 (Above) Gleaming red fur relies on wet-glowing techniques. Dry glows are used to soften and lighten fur, but they won't sufficiently lift the color for brilliant highlights. Working one glow at a time, be sure to leave a soupy-painty ring around wet Q-tip glow areas and re-brush them immediately, before the moisture evaporates.

Re-Brush and Groom

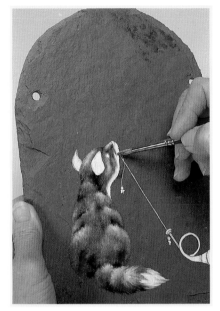

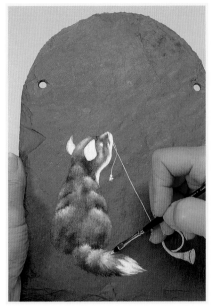

10 At this point, you'll need to remoisten your bristle brush often with gel to create smooth color transitions and to hold individual hair marks. You may have to paint, rough-brush, glow and re-brush an area several times if you miscalculated the paint load or overbrushed the area. For really vibrant highlights, there must be enough yellow paint under the glow. Adequate gel in the brush and liquid in the Q-tip make the fur glisten. Keep experimenting; keep re-doing. This really is no-fail painting!

11 You may want to add some white paint to the most brilliant highlights with a filbert rake.

12 Some areas may require deeper color. Add dark color directly with a bristle brush and blend in.

Adding Details

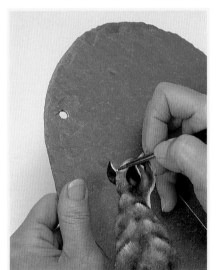

14 Paint the red cord and add black and yellow accents and details.

13 Paint the eyelashes, nose, mouth and tail markings black. Paint the ears with heavy paint and brush with a tickle touch so they stay very black. Glow the ear bases and brush in Burnt Sienna for shading. Add a fringe of white ear fur.

15 Clean up imperfections with a wet brush lift-out. It's easy on slate!

Painting Brass and Letters

Painting shining metal isn't difficult—just keep most reflections very sharp.

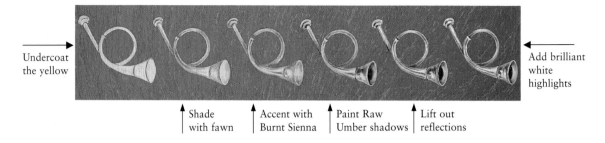

Undercoat the yellow →

← Add brilliant white highlights

↑ Shade with fawn   ↑ Accent with Burnt Sienna   ↑ Paint Raw Umber shadows   ↑ Lift out reflections

Carefully trace and transfer names or numbers in lettering of your choice. I chose the Raphael font because the curves of the letters echo the curve of the horn and the top of the slate. Pay particular attention to spacing. Not all letters are equidistant from each other. "Weight" the type for better flow and composition.

Shade your letters using whatever technique you feel most comfortable using: blending, double-loading or floating. We want your best!

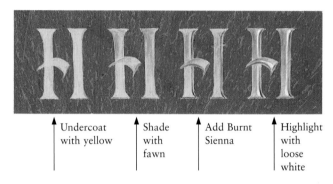

↑ Undercoat with yellow   ↑ Shade with fawn   ↑ Add Burnt Sienna   ↑ Highlight with loose white

Add Grasses

16 Freehand some grasses in basic green. Make blades come to life with yellow and white accents. Airplane the brush for tapered blades.

Completing Your Project

17 Varnish with satin water-based varnish. **Caution:** Do not sand between the first and second coats of varnish; you could damage the delicate raised fur lines. Then wax your slate. The colors will be even more vibrant than when you painted them, and every hair will spring to life! Use exterior varnish if the slate will be outside. If you wish, replace the rawhide hanger with a silken cord and tassels. Secure them well, because the slate is heavy and if it falls it *will* break.

Take a minute to admire your fox. You have painted one of nature's most gorgeous animals, and though it may have been a strange and circuitous route, you've outfoxed red fur!

(Below) Small oval slates used for door or horse stall plates complete the farm theme.

5

Hopping Down the Bunny Trail

You'll love painting these bunny baskets! There's something for all the

different artists within each of us: bunnies for the nature artist

and an egg and nest for our still-life side. Best of all,

there's lots of painting to do and none of it's too difficult.

What You'll Need

- Medium oval basket from Bentwood
- OR: Small strawberry basket from Bentwood
- OR: Goose egg from Cabin Crafters
- Wood preparation and finishing materials (including gesso)
- Base-coating materials
- Pale peachy pink acrylic paint for base coat
- Warm White acrylic paint for cameo base coats
- Acrylic flower and stripe colors: Warm White, pale peachy pink, Portrait, Hauser Green Medium
- X-Acto knife
- Heavy coated card stock or stencil blank for oval cameo stencil
- Krylon #1311 Matte Finishing Spray
- Mechanical pencil
- Tracing paper
- Grey transfer paper
- Angled brush and white acrylic paint for undercoating
- Scotch Magic Tape
- Piece of brown paper bag
- Q-tips and soft paper towels
- Brushes—tiny round hair, small bright hair, medium bright hair, small bristle round, medium bristle round, small filbert rake, small mop

OIL SUPPLIES
Gel medium, odorless thinner, white, Ivory Black, Raw Umber, Cadmium Yellow Light, Burnt Sienna, Sap Green, Vermilion Permanent, Prussian Blue. Mix these colors: soft brown, light brown, pink, light egg blue, egg blue, light basic greens.

ACRYLIC SUPPLIES
Gel medium, water, floating medium (optional), Wicker White, Pure Black, Raw Umber, Medium Yellow, Burnt Sienna, True Burgundy, Hauser Green Dark, Hauser Green Light, Red Light, Prussian Blue. Mix these colors: soft brown, light brown, pink, light egg blue, egg blue, light basic greens.

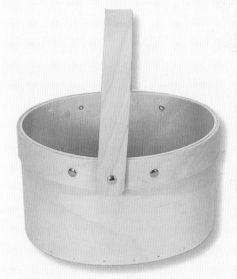

Preparing Your Surface

Sand and otherwise prepare your oval basket for painting. Gessoing is recommended. Base-coat the basket and handle with pale peachy pink, and the rim, interior, and handle underside with Warm White.

Begin With the Cameos

 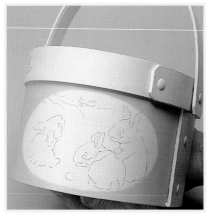 

1 Cut a stencil for the oval cameos. Base-coat the cameos with Warm White, stroking the paint away from the rim toward the middle of the oval to avoid leakage and buildup under the stencil. The side cameos should be spaced about 1½" from the center cameo. Smooth with a piece of heavy brown paper bag and mist the basket with Krylon #1311 Matte Finishing Spray to keep it impervious to dirt and paint smudges.

2 Trace and then transfer the design with grey transfer paper. Use a mechanical pencil and tread lightly: Transfer lines can be difficult to cover. Trace only as much as you'll need to find the pattern. Place the mother bird on the rim above the gap between the two cameos.

3 This is a very light background, and you may not need to undercoat much unless the surface has become overly slick. White fur areas must be undercoated, however. Gel and add pink to the ears. Lift out pink and blend in white paint for highlighting.

Paint the Shadows and Darks

4 These are tiny animals and require very little paint. Paint delicately and accurately, being extra careful when brown paint defines another shape. Keep your eye on what you're *not* painting. *Gel your surface* and then paint shadows and dark fur with a tiny bright brush and soft brown paint. Move to the transparent-looking strokes as your brush unloads. Soften the brown ear canals with a dry Q-tip, leaving one side darker.

5 With a tiny bright brush and loose squiggly strokes, scrumble in light brown in open areas. It should look transparent. Leave some background showing.

This pattern may be hand-traced or photocopied for personal use only. The pattern is shown full size.

The Fur Pattern

6 These are fluffy baby bunnies, so I've made the fur resemble a powder puff with lots of "tips only" showing as the hairs stand out from the body. As you compare the fur diagram to the rough brush below and the finished painting on page 67, think not only about the length and direction of the fur, but also about how the fur feels. Mentally hold the tiny body in your hands, run your fingers through the incredibly soft fur and imagine a soft spring breeze ruffling it. Your art will be better for having done this simple exercise.

Rough-Brush the Fur

7 Now, having "held" the bunnies, gently begin to brush the fur with a back-and-forth stroke. Pull out fine edge fur with a filbert rake. Wipe and re-gel your bristle brush frequently as you think "fluffy" and brush layers of fur on your babies. As with a lot of newborns, they don't look too cute at this stage to anyone but the parent. That's OK. *You* know they're going to be precious.

Glow Some Areas

8 With a dry Q-tip, glow the large, obvious glow areas first. Once these are established, it will be easier to place smaller glows. Very little wet-glowing is needed in this design. It is probably best to wet-glow only after the dry glows have been re-brushed, and then only in a few spots. Fuzzy fur reflects less light than sleek fur and doesn't require as much bright highlighting.

9 Lift out tiny glow areas with a brush. Now is a good time to clean up tails, muzzles and surrounding eye fur with a wet brush.

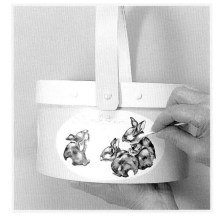

Re-Brush and Groom

10 Starting at the outer rim of each glowed area, carefully re-brush toward the center. Keep your bristle brush clean and re-moistened with gel. On slick surfaces, the longer you gently brush in back-and-forth strokes, the prettier the fur becomes (unlike working on canvas). Use no pressure, or the paint will lift off and leave a hole, not a glow!

Choose which highlights will retain bright centers, and on the others, brush through the centers for hazier glows. Too many bright highlights create a "polka-dot" composition.

Finishing Your Bunnies

11 Correct the color levels in the fur by adding paint directly with your bristle brush. Blend in gently.

Paint and shade the muzzles and paws with pink and white. Tracing lines tend to show through if you paint beyond them; so clean up paint that extends beyond them with a wet brush.

Fluff the tails with a bristle brush and enhance them with white paint. Pull out the tail edge fur with a small filbert rake, wiping the brush clean after each stroke. Add pink and brown with the rake to give the fur depth.

12 Add pinks, whites and touches of Burnt Sienna to the fur with a bristle brush for even softer, fuzzier baby fur. Paint the eyes with a tiny round brush heavily loaded with Raw Umber. Let the paint fall off the brush and then stir the puddle until it is the correct shape. Lift out eyelids with a tiny brush. The line left at the top of the lid will automatically be shaded and finer than if you painted it. Finish the eye with a sparkling white highlight. Three tiny whisker dots (there's hardly room for realism here), a few whiskers scratched out with an X-Acto knife, and your bunnies are ready to romp.

Completing the Cameos

13 Tree branches and vines shade effortlessly if you use a small bright brush loaded with gel and then dipped in various shades of brown. Due to the gel, the middle of the branch will be lighter and the branch will appear round. The gel also facilitates a realistic look as one branch or vine lies over another. Freehand small spring leaves in light shades of basic green. Be watchful of the composition you are creating.

Final Details

Building a Nest

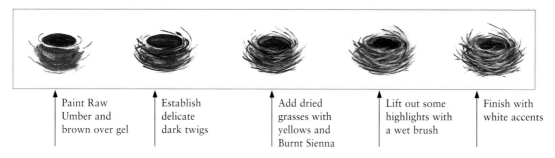

↑ Paint Raw Umber and brown over gel

↑ Establish delicate dark twigs

↑ Add dried grasses with yellows and Burnt Sienna

↑ Lift out some highlights with a wet brush

↑ Finish with white accents

The Egg and Grass

Follow these steps for painting the egg and freehanding the grass.

Gel and paint with light egg blue ↓

Shade with egg blue ↓

Lift out highlight, add white and blend ↓

Paint speckles with gelled soft brown ↓

↑ Paint tufts of grass with a small filbert rake

↑ Add basic green accents with a tiny round brush

↑ Establish tuft base and lift out blades with a small bright brush

The Mother Bird

Remember, a small bright lift-out brush is your best ally when painting tiny things.

↑ Gel and paint browns and Burnt Sienna

↑ Brush with a small bristle brush or rake

↑ Add pinks and whites

↑ Paint a yellow beak and a black eye

Finishing Your Project

14 Mask off the striping on the rim and handle of your basket with Scotch Magic Tape. Rub your fingers over the tape to make sure it has totally adhered. Seal the taped stripe with clear varnish or a coat of base-coat color. With acrylic color, paint a pale peachy pink stripe on the rim and a Warm White stripe on the handle. Remove the tape immediately and clean up any imperfections with a clean small bright brush and water.

Mark off the overall flower pattern with a dot at the center of each flower. Paint the flowers and leaves with a tiny round brush using simple comma strokes. The centers of the Warm White flowers are Portrait; the leaves, Hauser Green Medium.

Begin freehand vining the cameo and stripes with a single vine which establishes the flow the of the pattern. Use varying proportions of gel and soft brown in a small bright brush.

Entwine a second vine to further define the basic design. Then go back and embellish the vines with smaller growths and branching tendrils. Paint tiny leaves in varying hues of basic green.

15 Apply several coats of water-based satin varnish. **Caution:** Do not sand between the first and second coats of varnish; you could damage the delicate raised fur lines. When the varnish is dry, wax and buff the basket. Waxing really brings out the best in fur! Tie a bow on the handle for an added touch.

Your bunnies are now safely held in time and space for generations to come. If you put love in, love will surely come out!

6
Bluer Than Blue

White Persian cats are truly elegant creatures, in both appearance and personality. It seems only fitting to surround them with blue silk ribbons and paint them on a vanity set for a favorite "princess."

Preparing Your Surface

Sand and prepare your powder box. Several coats of gesso are well worth the trouble for this elegant design. Base-coat the lid top and underside rim with Wicker White. Base-coat the raised center portion on the underside of the lid with blue-grey, as well as the box's bottom, lower edge and interior. The remainder of the box is base-coated in Wicker White.

Mist the lid and box with Krylon #1311 Matte Finishing Spray to protect it.

What You'll Need

- 6″ diameter powder box from Allen's Wood Crafts
- OR: 6″×12″ round mirror from Allen's Wood Crafts
- Wood preparation and finishing materials (including gesso)
- Base coating materials
- Wicker White acrylic paint for base coat
- Blue-grey acrylic paint for background and stripes
- Krylon #1311 Matte Finishing Spray
- Mechanical pencil or stylus
- Tracing paper
- Grey transfer paper
- X-Acto knife
- ½″ Scotch Magic Tape
- Piece of heavy brown paper bag
- Q-tips and soft paper towels
- Lift-out tool (optional)
- Brushes—tiny round hair, small bright hair, medium bright hair, small bristle round, medium bristle round, small filbert rake, small mop

OIL SUPPLIES
Gel medium, odorless thinner, drying medium (optional), white, Ivory Black, Vermilion Permanent, Prussian Blue. Mix these colors: pink, basic blue-grey, dark blue-grey, deep blue-black.

ACRYLIC SUPPLIES
Gel medium, water, floating medium (optional), white, Pure Black, Red Light, Prussian Blue. Mix these colors: pink, basic blue-grey, dark blue-grey, deep blue-black.

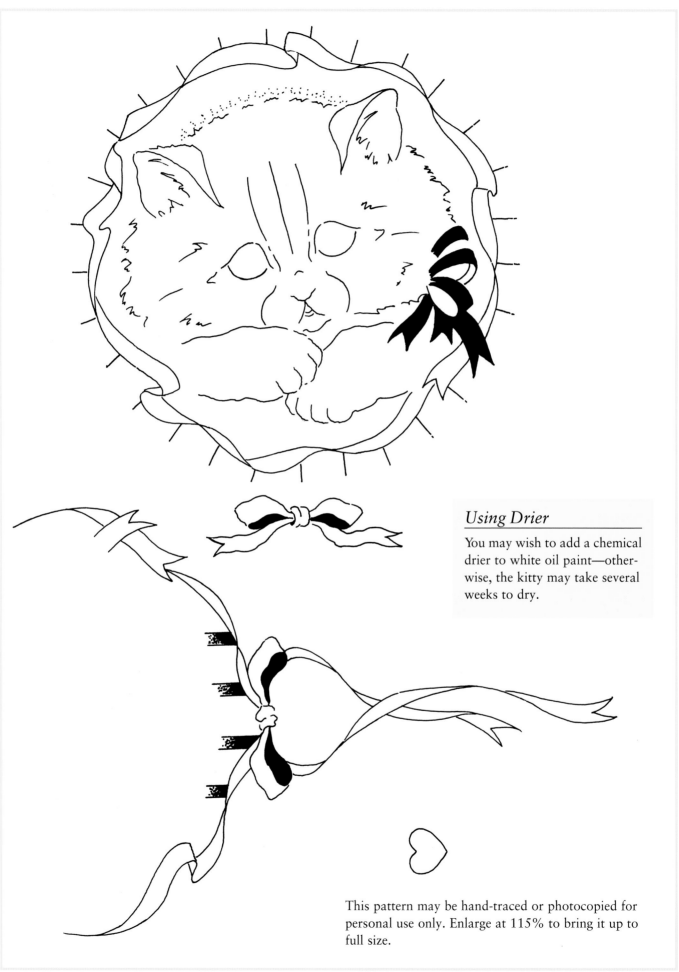

Using Drier

You may wish to add a chemical drier to white oil paint—otherwise, the kitty may take several weeks to dry.

This pattern may be hand-traced or photocopied for personal use only. Enlarge at 115% to bring it up to full size.

Before You Paint

1 Trace and then transfer the design with grey transfer paper as lightly as possible. The lighter, the better—and the less you'll have to cover later.

Undercoat the background inside the ribbons and behind the kitty with blue-grey, feathering the blue-grey into the area of the kitty's fur. (You may skip ahead and shade this background now or wait until later.) Undercoating the kitty should not be necessary unless the surface has become too slick with Krylon.

2 *Paint gel* on the ears and then paint the ears pink. Your pink should be a bit darker than usual to allow for lightening later, when white fur is stroked in.

With a dry Q-tip, lift out and shade the pink ear tips. Put pink on the nose and mouth so they won't get lost as you work.

Paint Shadows and Add Color

3 *Spread gel* over as much of the kitty as you'll be working on at one time. Heavily load a medium bright brush with dark blue-grey and paint dark shadow areas first, stroking in the general direction the fur grows. As the brush unloads, move to the lighter, more transparent-looking strokes.

4 Fill in the open spaces with gloppy, thick white paint. This is a good time to contemplate the fact that to achieve the illusion of form in light animals, you need many more darks than you might think.

The Fur Pattern

5 Study the fur diagram at right and compare it to the finished kitty on page 77. Long-haired kittens have short fur on their paws, outer ears and faces. Even where the fur is very long, it is composed of hundreds of layers. The fluffier the fur, the more layers of hair tips we see as the fur springs away from the body. The fur inside the ear grows not only out of the head, but from the sides of the ears.

Start the Rough Brush

6 With a medium bristle brush, brush the fur in white areas first, using a very light back-and-forth stroke. In these early stages the paint will be very "slip-slidey," and the back-and-forth motion will not only help maintain correct light and shadow shapes, but will also redistribute or remove paint to a manageable amount. Stipple the ears and muzzle.

Blend the blue-grey areas very gently, constantly wiping your brush clean. Since the paint is so deep, you'll probably not need to keep gel in the brush as yet. Occasionally, you may have to add more paint to an area.

Use Filbert Rake to Paint Fur

7 Use a filbert rake to pat a fringe of fur on the outer ear rims. Heavily load the rake with white and then paint feathery fur inside the ears. Be sure to airplane the brush.

8 Extend edge fur with a filbert rake and no pressure. If the wispy white paint strokes won't cover the background demarcation, repaint some blue-grey on the area and extend white hair tips over the wet blue-grey using a very light touch.

9 Final color adjustments are best added and blended in with a filbert rake. Check your "coal-bin" kitty. She looks dirty, but all her features and fur tufts should be in place.

Glow and Re-Brush

10 Varying pressures and a jiggling motion are the secrets to successful glowing. If you "scrub the sink" with the Q-tip, you create holes and destroy an entire range of values.

With the photos as your guide, glow and re-brush one or two areas at a time. Begin with the large, easy areas, then fill in with the less significant glows.

You may have to glow and re-brush an area several times. Just as in real life, Persian kittens need lots of grooming and stroking!

11 With gel in your bristle brush, carefully re-brush each glowed area. Wipe and re-gel your brush often. Repeat the glow-and-re-brush process until soft fur emerges (usually just before you're ready to give up). This destroying and replacing layers of paint may seem futile, but you are ultimately creating more realistic fur than a single application of paint could achieve. Also, the combination of white paint and the bare exposed surface makes for softer-looking fur than either could alone.

A feather-light "dusting" of the fur with a mop brush will remove any harsh stroke lines, and gossamer fur will materialize like magic!

Finishing Your Kitty's Fur

 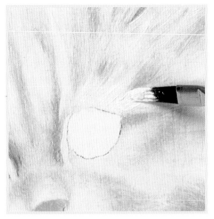 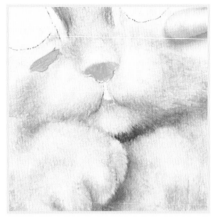

12 Adjust deep shadows with very dark paint. Don't be shy! Deep-value areas on white animals indicate only that not much light is able to reach the area—not that the animal is less than white.

13 Paint the fur surrounding the eyes with a filbert rake. Search for other areas where you can either paint additional hairs or extend existing fur with a clean rake.

14 Add pink under each eye and on the paws. With a dry Q-tip, soften the pink areas to a blush. This touch of color not only furthers the illusion of a baby animal, but also warms the cool blues and whites of the design amazingly.

"Dust" once more with a mop brush, and your kitty's fur is done!

Bringing Your Kitty to Life

Creating luminous eyes and an expression of innocent bewilderment is only steps away. But first, put the expression on your own face. That's right! Believe it or not, the kitty will mirror you. It's an old trick, but it works.

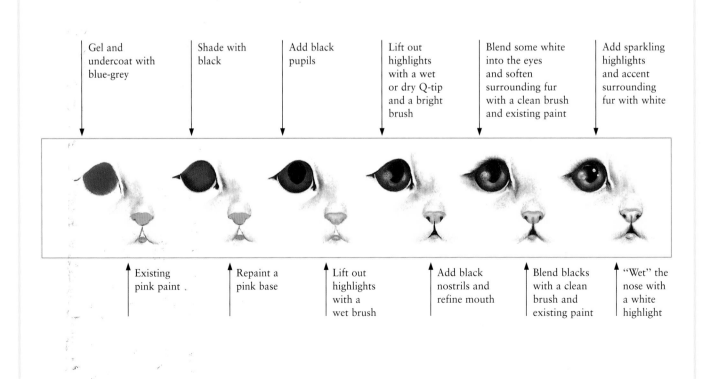

Gel and undercoat with blue-grey

Shade with black

Add black pupils

Lift out highlights with a wet or dry Q-tip and a bright brush

Blend some white into the eyes and soften surrounding fur with a clean brush and existing paint

Add sparkling highlights and accent surrounding fur with white

Existing pink paint

Repaint a pink base

Lift out highlights with a wet brush

Add black nostrils and refine mouth

Blend blacks with a clean brush and existing paint

"Wet" the nose with a white highlight

Finishing the Lid

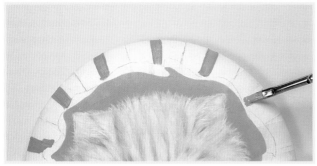

15 Trace and transfer the stripe lines for the lid. (Transferring is unnecessary on the base, since taping correctly will result in a perfect pattern.)

Place a ½" piece of Scotch Magic Tape along each side of the stripe line, ¹⁄₁₆" from the line. This will mask off a ⅛" stripe of surface ready for painting. Tape off every other stripe in this manner. Rub down all tape edges to insure good adherence. Seal the taped stripes with a coat of clear varnish or Wicker White.

Paint each stripe, using as many coats as needed, with blue-grey acrylic paint. Clean up any paint that strays into the ribbon area with a wet brush. Also, check the underside of the lid periodically for any stray paint.

After every few stripes, remove the tape and clean up any imperfections with a wet bright brush. When the painted stripes are dry, tape the remaining alternate stripes and paint them in the same manner.

16 Highlight and shade the background with white and deeper blues. Float or blend paint as you choose. (A mop is indispensable for blending in oil.) Be sure to pull fur back over the background if necessary.

Again, use techniques you feel comfortable with for the best results. These ribbons were painted and then blended with a tiny mop. Edges were cleaned and sharpened by lifting out drifted paint with a medium bright wet brush. You may prefer to float or double-load.

Edge loops are easily painted with a dab of paint on the point of a lift-out tool.

Repaint fur over the neck ribbon to sink the ribbon into the deep fur. Paint whisker dots; add whiskers and eyebrow hairs with a sharp X-Acto knife. If you're a real sentimentalist like me, paint an indication of a tiny tear under one eye.

Paint the ribbon using this guideline.

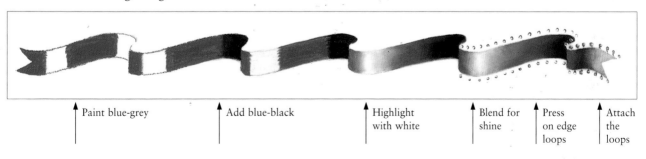

| ↑ Paint blue-grey | ↑ Add blue-black | ↑ Highlight with white | ↑ Blend for shine | ↑ Press on edge loops | ↑ Attach the loops |

Finishing the Box

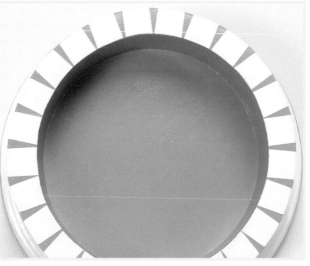

17 On the base of the box, paint the ribbon before striping to prevent the stripe ridges from showing through the ribbon. With ½″ Scotch Magic Tape, mask off all the stripes on the box. Place each length of tape ⅛″ apart from the preceding length. You should come out perfectly at the "finish line," or you will with some minor repositioning. Seal and then paint the stripes, immediately removing any excess paint on the ribbon with a wet bright brush.

18 Use tape lengths long enough to lap over the rim of the box. The resulting pattern will echo the sunburst design of the lid.

Completing Your Project

19 Apply several coats of water-based satin varnish. **Caution:** Do not sand between the first and second coats of varnish; you could damage the delicate raised fur lines. Be sure to wax this project. Waxing will not only enhance the beauty of the kitty fur, but will prevent the lid from sticking to the base, especially in warm climates.

If you wish, add a music box—maybe one that plays "Memory" from *Cats*. Perhaps a blue-bowed, ostrich-feather powder puff is the final touch you're seeking. Nothing is too fancy for a princess, human or kitten!

If you are painting your kitty on the mirror, the ribbon circle will need to be slightly larger than for the powder box. The kitty is the same size.

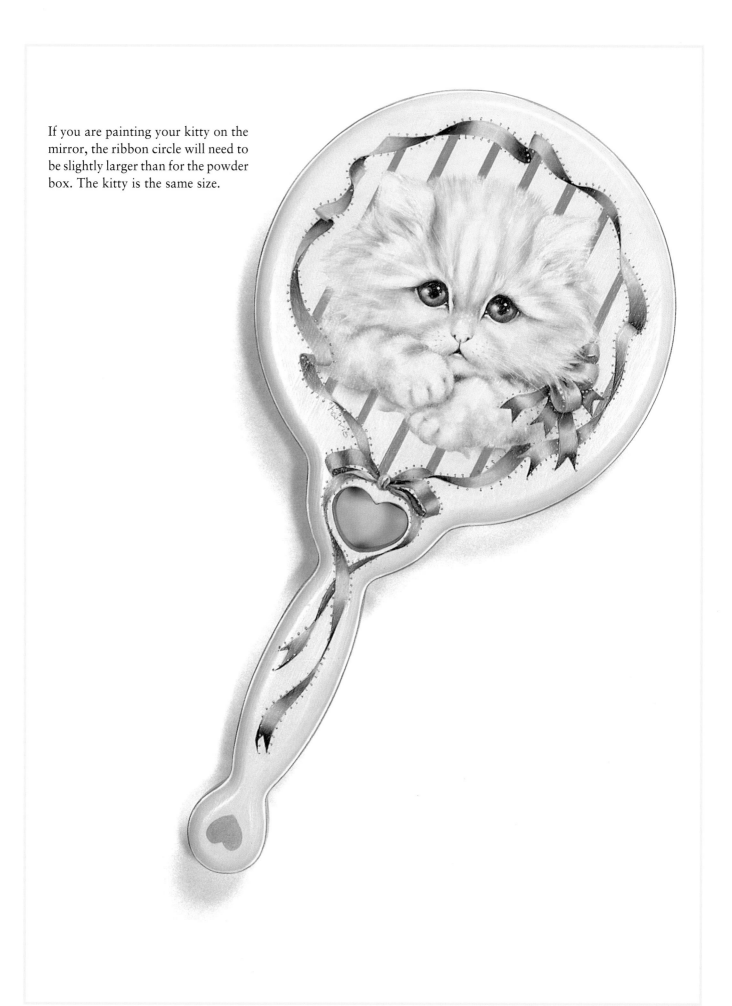

7
Just Looking!

One of the best parts of being an animal artist is watching

your subjects. We had an ancient tree in the yard that was home to

raccoons, squirrels and a great horned owl. Sometimes a tree is a whole

apartment house, and you never know who's moving in next.

Preparing Your Surface

Just as every tree is unique, the rounds cut from them also vary considerably. Select your round before sizing the pattern, visualizing the design on the round. Some discolorations or imperfections in the wood can be incorporated into the design. Others cannot, so choose accordingly.

After you have sanded and sealed your country round, mist the round with Krylon #1311 Matte Finishing Spray. Be careful with the natural bark rim as you work on this project, as it can chip off.

What You'll Need

- 10½″ basswood country round from Walnut Hollow
- OR: Candle box from Walnut Hollow
- Wood preparation and finishing materials
- Krylon #1311 Matte Finishing Spray
- Mechanical pencil or stylus
- Tracing paper
- Transfer paper—grey and white
- Angled brush and white acrylic paint for undercoating
- X-Acto knife
- Scotch Magic Tape
- Piece of heavy brown paper bag
- Q-tips, soft paper towels and cotton balls
- Pieces of synthetic or natural sponge
- Brushes—tiny round hair, small bright hair, medium bright hair, small bristle round, medium bristle round, small filbert rake, small mop

OIL SUPPLIES
Gel medium, odorless thinner, white, Ivory Black, Raw Umber, Cadmium Yellow Light, Burnt Sienna, Sap Green, Prussian Blue. Mix these colors: various shades of basic green, adding white, yellow, black and Prussian Blue.

ACRYLIC SUPPLIES
Gel medium, water, floating medium (optional), white, Pure Black, Raw Umber, Medium Yellow, Burnt Sienna, Sap Green, Prussian Blue. Mix these colors: various shades of basic green, adding white, yellow, black and Prussian Blue.

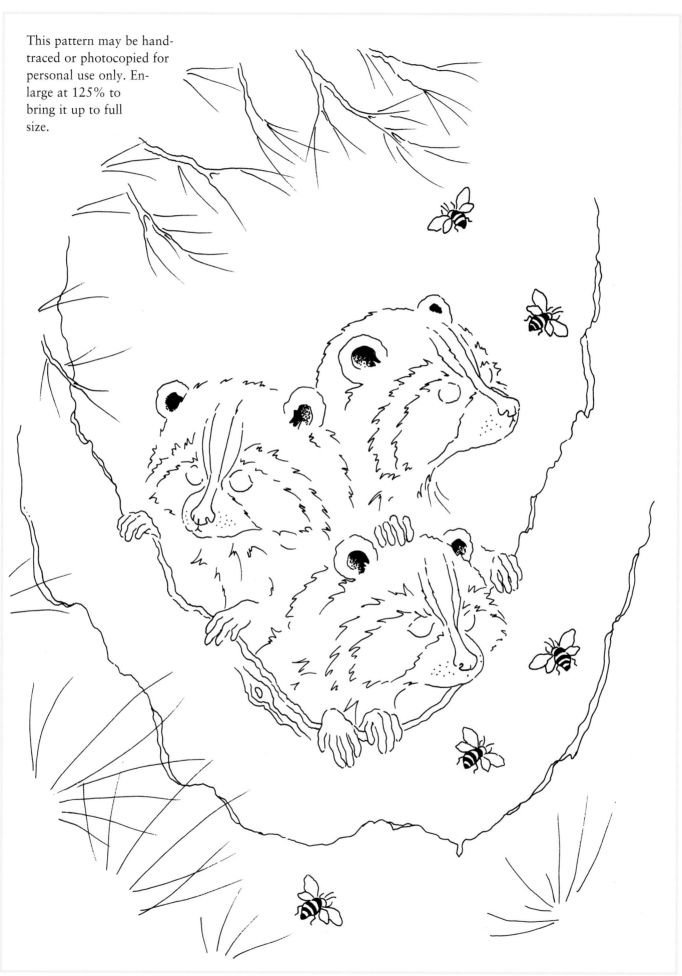

This pattern may be hand-traced or photocopied for personal use only. Enlarge at 125% to bring it up to full size.

Start With Faces and Ears

1 Trace and transfer the basic design with grey transfer paper. Alter the pattern as necessary to fit your round. Some elements, such as bees and tree branches, will be transferred later with white transfer paper.

Undercoat the eyes, ears and white facial fur with white acrylic paint. Use an angled brush to feather the fur.

You may choose to paint the dark hole at this point, or wait until your raccoons are completed.

2 *Gel the areas* you'll be painting. Begin by painting some Raw Umber in the middle of the eye or nose. Heavily load a small bright brush with black. Painting directly over the Raw Umber, enlarge the painted area until it almost covers the shape. With a tiny round brush (and no new paint), stretch the existing paint to the final edges of the shape. Make sure your eye shapes are perfect before proceeding.

With a medium bright brush, apply heavy black paint in the mask, staying slightly away from the eye rims. With a tiny round brush and existing paint, gradually shove the paint ahead of the brush until it reaches the white rims. Sneak up just a bit at a time for perfect results.

Note

It is probably wise to complete the top two raccoons before painting the bottom one, so your hand won't accidentally mess up the lower baby.

This pattern may be hand-traced or photocopied for personal use only. Enlarge at 122% to bring it up to full size.

Paint Shadows and Add Color

3 With a heavily loaded bright brush, finish painting the black mask. Next, paint deep shadow areas and the black markings above the white of the mask. Finish the dark head fur with strokes painted in the general direction the fur grows.

4 Randomly scrumble Raw Umber into empty spaces. Try to ride the paint on top of the underlying gel so that it remains fairly opaque rather than transparent.

5 Heavily load a bright brush with white and paint the ears and face. The paint should be deep and gloppy-looking, almost as if the white areas had been hit with a cream pie.

The Fur Pattern

6 Study this fur diagram well before you rough-brush your raccoons. In particular, note the rotating angles of the facial fur as it sweeps away from the eyes and over the face toward the neck. As you compare the diagram to the rough-brush photo on the next page and the finished painting on page 87, observe the varying lengths of fur, from the extremely short, smooth muzzle fur to the long "Sylvester cat" fur of the cheeks.

Rough-Brush the Fur

7 Moisten your bristle brush with gel and begin brushing the dark head fur first. Wipe out and re-gel the brush often to maintain black and brown color variations. Add more color if needed.

Stipple the short, white fur of the ears and muzzle, allowing some dark paint to travel into areas you want shaded. With no pressure, using an airplane stroke, brush the white facial markings into the dark fur.

Wipe the brush clean after every stroke. When you're finished, carefully drag some dark shading from the head fur into the white.

Brush the black mask into the white fur, wiping the brush clean after every stroke. Stay away from the white eye rims as you finish the mask. Your bristle brush might mess them up, and besides, it's so dark around these beady eyes, you wouldn't be able to see individual hairs anyway!

Finishing the Fur

8 Raccoons have fur with grey and brown color along each hair shaft. Create the look of this grizzled fur with a mixture of white and gel applied over the dark fur with a bristle brush and no pressure. Use the finished painting photo on page 87 as your guide. Frequently clean and reload the brush, or the paint will mush and you'll have a very old and grey raccoon.

9 Glow some areas of the fur with a dry Q-tip for soft highlights and color variation. Re-brush with a bristle brush and enough gel to hold the hair marks.

Continue lifting paint, adding paint and re-brushing with a bristle brush or a filbert rake until you've created soft baby raccoon fur.

10 Refine white fur with a filbert rake, wiping the brush clean after every stroke.

It's easy to become so involved with the white fur that it stretches up to the ears before you know it. Hold the shape of the face markings by brushing dark fur back into the white.

Dust the fur with a small mop for a really silky look.

Bring the Personality to Life

Imagine the personality of each baby raccoon. Is one shy and one a troublemaker? Is one a prankster, another bewildered? You decide. Think about each personality as you paint it. And put the expression on your own face as you work—it helps!

11 (Top left) Lift out the nose and iris highlights with a dry bright brush. (Float painted highlights if the eye has dried.)

12 (Top right) Blend yellow and Burnt Sienna into the eyes and glow again with a wet bright brush.

13 (Bottom left) Add white highlights, letting the paint fall off the brush. Blend the nose highlights with a clean brush.

14 (Bottom right) Paint whisker dots and pouty mouths. (Stick out your chin!) Soften the dots and mouths with a clean, dry brush.

Painting Paws

Just like human hands, raccoon paws can be difficult to paint. Use your own knuckles and finger pads as a reference. Don't get frustrated. You can clean up, repaint and reshape anything in this method. Cute paws are bound to emerge sooner or later!

15 Paint the paws with black and Raw Umber loaded together in a small bright brush.

16 Lift out knuckles and highlights with a clean, dry small bright brush.

17 Add white paint to the highlights and stroke the paws with a clean filbert rake to create fur. *Vaguely* indicate claws—after all, these are babies.

Faux Wood on Real Wood

Faux-finishing wood on real wood is fun and fast because nature's already done most of the work for you. Take a minute to decide which of your country round's features you wish to enhance. Each round you paint will be slightly different depending on your special creativity in using the following techniques.

PAINTING THE HOLE

Rotting wood inside old trees creates a warm hidey-hole for animals. Experiment with these techniques to create a snuggly home for your baby raccoons.

Note

This is messy, so you may wish to make a shield to protect your babies. If you do damage some of the edge fur, either clean it or repaint it with a filbert rake.

As you work, store your sponge pieces in water to keep them pliable (even if you are working with oil paint and thinner). Always blot excess moisture on a paper towel pad before using a sponge.

18 Paint random stripes of Raw Umber and Burnt Sienna. Some yellow may occasionally be added to the Burnt Sienna.

19 Dip the blotted sponge in water (for acrylic) or thinner (for oil), squeeze it out and place the sponge on the paint stripes. Gently wiggle the sponge in place for a moment to release moisture onto the paint. Lift off the sponge to reveal a pattern of rough wood. If you wish, blot with a paper towel for more lifting.

20 Dip a clean, damp sponge in a bit of paint and sponge on some speckles. Soften the patterns you've made with a small mop using horizontal and vertical strokes.

PAINTING THE WOOD

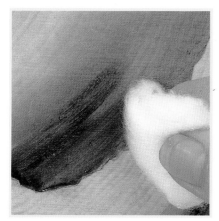

21 Spread gel over areas to be shaded. Paint the area with Raw Umber, then blend the paint with a dry cotton ball.

22 Accent existing ring patterns with gelled Raw Umber and a small bright brush. Haze the rings with a mop.

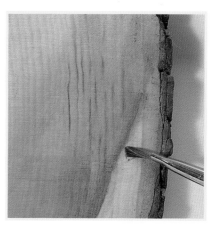

23 Clean up and sharpen edges of the rings with a wet medium bright brush.

Finishing the Illusion

24 Dip a damp sponge in Raw Umber to create speckled areas and stripes.

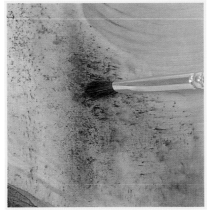

25 Brush the speckles with a clean, dry mop to create variations of texture and shading.

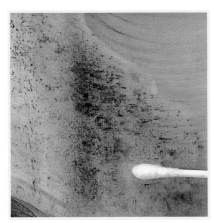

26 A dry Q-tip lifts out unwanted speckles or further blends the speckles.

27 Add a knothole (or enhance a real one) and you've completed the illusion!

The Rest of the Story

After your painting is dry, transfer bees and pine needles with white transfer paper.

Liberally paint white wings

Lightly press with your finger to create veins

Paint yellow and black stripes

Add Burnt Sienna shading and fuzz with a rake

Accent wing with black and highlight body with white

Finish details with black or Burnt Sienna

Final Touches

28 Paint tree branches with various shades of Raw Umber mixed with yellow or white. Delineate the branches with bright highlights.

Add sparse pine needles, always airplaning the brush for sharp, tapered tips. Brush-mix many shades of green as you work by pulling brown, blue, yellow or white into your basic green.

Control the size and number of needles you are creating so as not to make your composition top-heavy.

29 Scratch out twitchy whiskers on your raccoons with an X-Acto knife. Whiskers that do not show up sufficiently on the tree wood may be painted with white paint and then thinned to a fine line with a wet lift-out brush.

30 Several coats of varnish and an application of finishing wax really bring out the lustrous beauty of the wood and the raccoons' shining eyes and silky fur. Remember not to sand between the first and second coats of varnish; you could damage the delicate raised fur lines.

Now the only thing that's a mess is their personalities. These curious little ones are trouble just waiting to happen. And there's no way to gloss over that!

8

Circle of Love

I hope you'll explore the versatile world of "plaque art." Plaques of all shapes

and sizes can be decorated and then put on everything from large pieces

of furniture to tiny jewelry boxes. My creative streak goes wild with just

the thought of all these possibilities. I bet yours will too!

What You'll Need

- Child's chair from Crews' Country Pleasures
- 6″×6″ circle plaque from Crews' Country Pleasures
- Seven 1″ buttons from Crews' Country Pleasures
- Wood preparation/finishing materials (including gesso and wood glue)
- Base-coating materials
- Light cream acrylic paint for base coat
- Any small stencil to mark off decorative flower pattern (Hearts and Checks #28772 from Plaid/Simply Stencils works well)
- Pale peachy pink acrylic paint for striping
- Peachy pink acrylic paint for flowers
- Deep peach acrylic paint for flower centers
- Hauser Green Medium acrylic paint for stems and leaves
- Krylon #1311 Matte Finishing Spray
- Mechanical pencil or stylus
- Tracing paper
- Grey transfer paper
- Angled brush and white acrylic paint for undercoating
- Green Umber acrylic paint for background
- X-Acto knife
- Scotch Magic Tape
- Piece of brown paper bag
- Q-tips and soft paper towels
- Brushes—tiny round hair, small bright hair, medium bright hair, small bristle round, medium bristle round, small filbert rake, small mop

OIL SUPPLIES
Gel medium, odorless thinner, white, Ivory Black, Raw Umber, Cadmium Yellow Light, Burnt Sienna, Sap Green, Vermilion Permanent, Prussian Blue. Mix these colors: soft brown, fawn, pink, basic green, blue-grey.

ACRYLIC SUPPLIES
Gel medium, water, floating medium (optional), white, Pure Black, Raw Umber, Medium Yellow, Burnt Sienna, True Burgundy, Hauser Green Dark, Sap Green, Red Light, Prussian Blue. Mix these colors: soft brown, fawn, pink, basic green, blue-grey.

Preparing Your Surfaces

Plaques add architectural interest to a piece, and they provide an easily handled surface for painting fine detail work.

Sand and otherwise prepare your chair, checkers and plaque. If you wish, gesso the front of the chair back. Gesso the smooth side and rims of the checkers and the front of the plaque.

Base-coat all surfaces with a light cream color and mist with Krylon #1311 Matte Finishing Spray.

This pattern may be hand-traced or photocopied for personal use only. Enlarge at 105% to bring it up to full size.

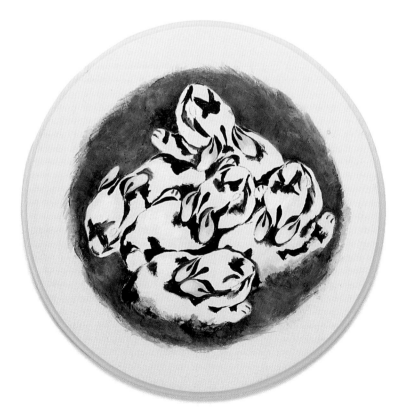

Begin Your Nest and Bunnies

1 Trace and cut out the circular pattern and transfer the design with grey transfer paper. *Gel* and then roughly block in the nest background with acrylic paint. Use either Green Umber and white or a mixture of greens, browns and white. Feather the edges and stipple the paint with a bristle brush to blend it.

Undercoat the ears, glow areas and white fur areas with white acrylic paint.

2 *Gel* and paint pink in the ears, carefully preserving the floppy, newborn shapes. Lift out the tips with a dry Q-tip and shade with white paint.

3 *Paint gel* over the area you'll be painting. This is a jumble of bunnies, so paint the shadows and darks methodically. Be particularly aware of paint strokes that define another shape such as a head or ear.

Using soft brown and a small bright brush, paint one bunny at a time. Carefully follow the pattern lines so that all the bunnies in the pile maintain their correct shapes.

4 Blend the brown ear canals with a dry Q-tip and no pressure.

Scrumble in Color

5 Loosely scrumble in gelled soft brown and some fawn. The paint should look transparent, and some background should still be visible.

The Fur Pattern

6 What confusion! Just keep saying, "Tip of the nose, over the head and down the tummy, out to the tail and paws!"

Remind yourself how incredibly soft and downy your newborn bunnies' fur feels.

Rough-Brush Your Bunnies

7 These are sleeping newborn babies. Try not to wake them! Work with a gentle touch to produce the delicate look you want.

Use a bristle brush in a short back-and-forth stroke. Wipe clean and re-gel your brush often to maintain the shadows that define each bunny.

Establish pretty edge fur, and adjust the color levels by adding paint with a bristle brush.

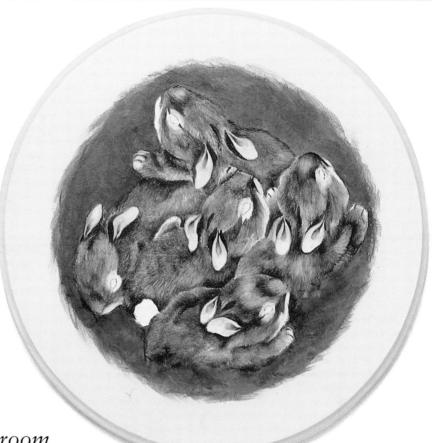

Glow, Re-Brush and Groom

8 Glow and re-brush one or two areas on one bunny at a time. Work large, obvious areas, such as the forehead, first. Some of the large glows will need both a dry and a wet Q-tip glow, but most of the glowing can be accomplished with dry Q-tips. Remove small glows, clean up, and redefine eyes, paws and muzzles with a wet bright brush.

9 Re-brush glowed areas with a gelled bristle brush and a gentle back-and-forth motion. Wipe out and re-gel the brush more frequently as you approach the center of a glow area to insure a smooth transition from dark to light. Some areas will have to be glowed repeatedly and re-brushed until the soft baby fur appears.

Add and blend white paint into some of the more prominent glowed areas and the tail.

Last, glow the brown ear fur.

Finishing Your Bunnies

Using the completed plaque photo on the next page as your guide, add the finishing touches to your baby bunnies.

10 Add and blend a hint of pink to the bunnies' fur with a small bristle brush.

11 Perfect the tiny ears using Q-tips, a filbert rake and a tiny round brush.

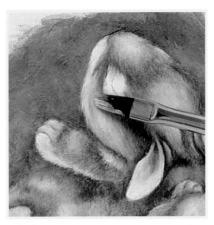

12 Paint the white paws and muzzle, brush with a filbert rake and add pink where appropriate.

13 Paint the eyelids, brush with a filbert rake and indicate the sleeping lid line. Add whisker dots and scratch off whiskers and eyebrow hairs with an X-Acto knife. Shhh . . . you made it!

Nestle the Bunnies

14 Spread gel on the nest and adjust the shading using greens, browns and whites. Begin the nest edge with grass blades of light browns and greens, pointing the grasses counterclockwise.

Finish the nest, one layer at a time. Brush-mix on your palette varying values and hues of paint as you work. Use any brush-loading or lifting-out techniques you are comfortable with to re-create this fragile spring scene.

Nesting Step by Step

Paint base grasses

Paint lighter grasses of white or light yellow in the wet background

Add light green and brown grasses

Paint a green base for the clover bloom

Paint white clover petals in the green base

Add pink flowers sparked with white

Paint a green clover leaf shape

Add white variegation

Paint pink flowers with yellow centers

Double-load green and white for large leaves

Add blue flowers sparked with white

Finish the Plaque and Buttons

15 Paint a pale peachy pink acrylic paint border on the beveled edge of the plaque and around the side of each button.

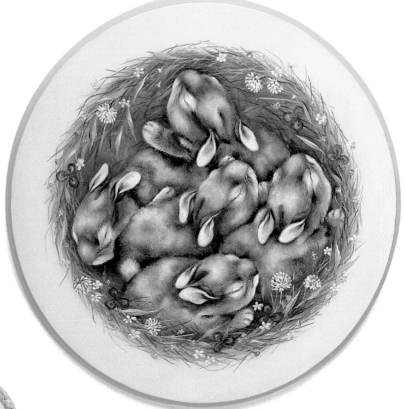

16 Trace and transfer the tiny bunnies with grey transfer paper. Paint the bunnies using the springtime bunnies in Project 5 on page 62 as your guide. When working in miniature, a wet tiny bright lift-out brush is invaluable. Often "cleaning up" is easier than painting perfectly!

Freehand mini-bouquets, meadows and floral borders using a tiny round brush and heavy paint. Then go rest your eyes!

Decorate the Chair

17 Buy or make a stencil to facilitate marking off the overall flower pattern. Plan your placement with care before you begin so that the pattern will fall on legs and rails accurately. Mark the center of each flower.

18 Paint the peachy pink flower petals in acrylic paint with a tiny round brush using comma strokes. Add deep peach centers and Hauser Green Medium stems and leaves. Some areas will be hard to reach. You'll have more control if you turn the chair upside down to work.

19 Flowers need not be perfectly matched, but they should be consistent in size and color level. And as long as you've done this much, why not decorate the underside of the seat? It's a nice finishing touch.

Putting It All Together

20 Mask off ¼″ stripes with Scotch Magic Tape. Extend the side stripe up and over the top of the chair. Rub the tape with your fingers to make sure it is tightly adhering to the surface along the stripe edges. Seal the taped stripes with clear varnish or cream base coat. Paint the stripes with pale peachy pink acrylic, working one section at a time. Successive coats may be necessary.

21 Before the last coat on a section dries, strip the tape and clean up any imperfections with a wet bright brush. Don't forget to stripe the opening between the seat and the back. It's a difficult space to get into, but the effort will pay off in the form of a beautifully finished piece.

Finish the Chair

22 Varnish your chair, plaque and buttons with several coats of water-based satin varnish. **Caution:** Do not sand between the first and second coats of varnish; you could damage the delicate raised fur lines. Choose a glue that will adhere well to painted surfaces and attach the plaque and buttons to your decorated chair.

You've created a family heirloom, so give it the hand-rubbed luster that only finishing wax provides. Painting a piece with this many design elements is always a challenge, but it's well worth the time and effort.

23 Take a moment to contemplate the generations to come who will treasure the chair you've painted. Now, that's a happy ending!

9

Kitty Catastrophe

Circles are an ideal format for animals in action. These surfaces almost begin to swirl as the kitties chase round and round. You may want your kitties chasing butterflies or yarn. You could even change their color to that of a favorite pet. It's your personal touches that make your work so special!

What You'll Need

- 10″ lidded basket from Pesky Bear
- 1³⁄₁₆″ × ⁷⁄₈″ spool from Cabin Crafters
- OR: Four-legged 10″ stool from Drake Distributors
- Wood preparation and finishing materials, including wood glue
- Base-coating materials
- Deep peach acrylic paint for base coat
- Mustard acrylic paint for base coat
- Wicker White acrylic paint for buttons and tape measure
- Deep peach acrylic paint for spool knob
- Krylon #1311 Matte Finishing Spray
- Tape measure
- Mechanical pencil or stylus
- Tracing paper
- Transfer paper—grey and white
- Angled brush and white acrylic paint for undercoating
- X-Acto knife
- Scotch Magic Tape
- #0000 synthetic steel wool pad or piece of brown paper bag
- Q-tips and soft paper towels
- Brushes—tiny round hair, small bright hair, medium bright hair, small bristle round, medium bristle round, small filbert rake, small mop

OIL SUPPLIES
Gel medium, odorless thinner, white, Ivory Black, Raw Umber, Cadmium Yellow Light, Burnt Sienna, Vermilion Permanent. Mix these colors: deep pink, deep peach.

ACRYLIC SUPPLIES
Gel medium, floating medium (optional), white, Pure Black, Raw Umber, Medium Yellow, Burnt Sienna, Red Light, Napthol Crimson. Mix these colors: deep pink, deep peach.

Preparing Your Surface

Since you will not base-coat most of this project, choose a basket and lid with attractive grain and even color. Sand, seal and otherwise prepare your basket and lid. Mist the lid with Krylon #1311 Matte Finishing Spray.

This pattern may be hand-traced or photocopied for personal use only. Enlarge at 133% to bring up to full size.

Undercoat and Add Pink

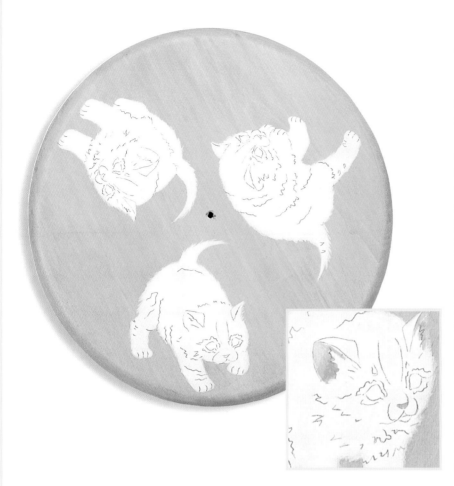

1 Trace and cut out the circular pattern. Transfer the outline of each kitty to the lid with white transfer paper.

Undercoat the kitties with white acrylic paint. Use an angled brush, and feather the fur edges as you work. Several coats will be needed for good coverage. Smooth the white paint with a synthetic steel wool pad or a piece of heavy brown paper bag. Dust with a tack cloth.

Transfer the interior patterns on each kitty with grey transfer paper. Keep the lines as light as possible, as they are difficult to cover when painting fluffy, long fur. Be particularly careful to transfer the faces accurately. It will save lots of work later!

2 Gel and paint the ears and noses with deep pink. With a Q-tip, highlight the top of the pink area, adding white paint if you wish.

Paint the Shadows and Darks

3 Gel the surface of only as much area as you'll be working on at one time. With a small bright brush, loosely paint in Raw Umber shadow areas. These areas will make more sense if you compare this paint pattern to the finished kitty on page 107.

Note

Many of the photos will show all three kitties being worked on at once. Even *I'm* not that fast or brave! Keep in mind that fur must be worked while it is still wet. What if the phone rings and your kitty fur dries up? It's much safer to work one kitty's fur, a part at a time, until that kitty's fur is totally finished, then move on to the next kitty.

Define Shapes With Shadows

4 Be very attentive to dark shadows that define another shape. The dark strokes behind the head determine the shape of the head. Likewise, darks may define the shape of an ear, muzzle or raised leg. Watch what you're *not* painting.

5 Other dark strokes define layers of fluff. Some strokes serve only to define the striped pattern of the kitty's fur.

6 The shadows are the foundation upon which you build realistic fur. Compare your kitties to these close-up photos once more to make sure you're off to a good start, because it's going to get wild!

Add Burnt Sienna and Yellow

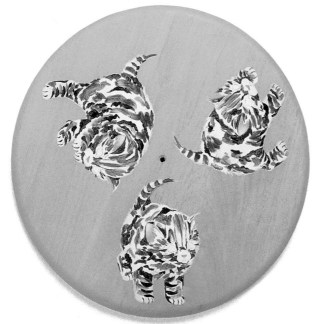 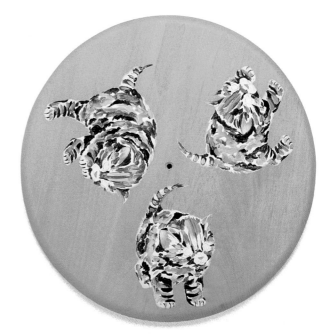

7 Scrumble Burnt Sienna in the open spaces of the pattern. Paint stripes on the tails. Try to ride the paint on top of the gelled surface by letting it fall off the brush. When brush hairs touch the surface, the paint mixes in the gel and becomes transparent. Leave some undercoating showing.

8 Load a medium bright brush heavily with yellow. Once again, let the paint fall off the brush as you paint. Distribute yellow over the kitty, even over Burnt Sienna areas. The yellow not only lends color to the fur, but is essential for the glow areas. Without yellow under the glows, the fur won't be luminous.

This looks pretty scary, but don't worry about it. Just move on to the next step. We've lots to do.

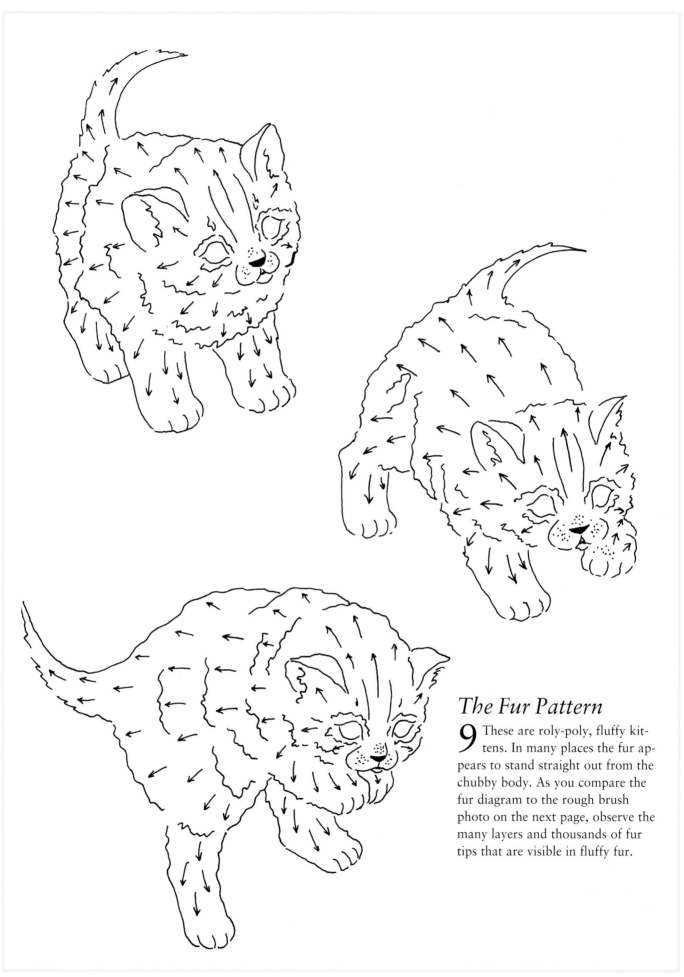

The Fur Pattern

9 These are roly-poly, fluffy kittens. In many places the fur appears to stand straight out from the chubby body. As you compare the fur diagram to the rough brush photo on the next page, observe the many layers and thousands of fur tips that are visible in fluffy fur.

Rough-Brush the Fur

10 With a medium bristle brush, a back-and-forth stroke and no pressure, brush the edge fur of the area you're working on. Airplane the brush for pretty fur tips. Perfect the edge fur with a filbert rake.

Then, methodically brush in the layers of the area, beginning with the layers farthest away from your eye.

11 Wipe clean and re-gel your brush often. You want to blend the color, not travel and mush it into a single color. Adjust any color levels in the fur that look weak. The kitties should have deep, rich color at this stage.

Glow Some Areas

12 Glow one or two areas at a time with a wet Q-tip. Re-brush the area while it is still wet, before proceeding to the next glow area. Make all glows larger than the final highlighted area.

13 Have a whole fistful of Q-tips wet and ready to use! You're going to need them because, to begin with, these kitties have lots of glowed fur areas. Then, you'll have to repeat many of those glows, and on top of that, in this bright color the Q-tips are good for only one swipe (or less).

Re-Brush and Groom

14 Re-brush and re-glow your kitties until the soft, fluffy fur appears. Remember, you can repeat and correct processes almost endlessly in this method. It doesn't matter so much what you did or how many times you did it, but rather, what it looks like.

When the fur looks almost finished, gently dust the kitties with a clean, dry small mop.

15 Check for any further color adjustment needed, including any dry Q-tip glowing that might enhance the fur. Blend white paint into some of the brightest glowed areas. Use a filbert rake to paint wispy ear, ruff and tail fur.

16 Paint the white fur around the eyes. Blend and feather the paint with a small filbert rake. Lift out and shade the sides of the muzzles with pink. Stipple with a bristle brush for easy blending.

Define the noses and mouths with Raw Umber, add whisker dots, and scratch off whiskers with an X-Acto blade. Whiskers that extend into the background will show up better if they are first painted and then refined with a wet lift-out brush.

Painting Eyes

Be particular when painting eyes. If something's less than perfect, fix it. After all, the eyes reflect the heart and soul of your baby animal.

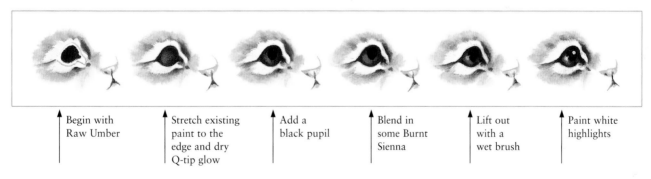

Begin with Raw Umber | Stretch existing paint to the edge and dry Q-tip glow | Add a black pupil | Blend in some Burnt Sienna | Lift out with a wet brush | Paint white highlights

Add the Details

17 Transfer the unwinding thread pattern with white transfer paper. Paint the thread with varying values of deep peach. Brush-mix the values in the palette as you work.

If you're not too steady painting long sweeping lines, don't fret. A quick fix with a wet lift-out brush, and you're back on track.

Faux Thread

I used a very old, real spool of thread on my basket. A faux spool is more durable, however, and lots of fun to paint.

Use very thick acrylic paint and a filbert rake to imitate the striations. Turn the spool gradually, letting the rake drag in the paint. As you paint threads, *move only the spool*, never the brush.

What appear to be the darkest shades on the spool are not painted, but the result of natural reflections on the curved surface.

Paint deep peach base coat with filbert rake

Paint lighter peach highlight stripes with filbert rake

Paint and blend white highlight stripes with filbert rake

Paint threads of white and light peach with tiny round brush

18 Position the spool on the basket lid as if one of the faux diagonal threads were winding off the spool and onto the basket. Glue the spool to the lid.

Complete Your Basket

19 Now your kitties are chasing the thread round and round the lid. You may prefer to have your kitties chasing yarn. Instead of the spool, use the round knob that comes with the basket. Faux-finish a yarn ball, and you've made a knitting basket.

20 Base-coat the basket's bottom, inside rim and handle with deep peach acrylic paint. Paint the outside of the rim and handle with a mustard color.

Using a real tape measure as a model, accurately replicate the measurements. You never know, it might come in handy!

With Wicker White and Raw Umber, randomly paint tiny shirt buttons around the rim. You can place the buttons so they cover small nail heads.

21 Varnish and wax your basket. **Caution:** Do not sand between the first and second coats of varnish; you could damage the delicate raised fur lines. If you are really energetic, add a pretty flowered chintz liner.

You may decide to use this basic design for an entirely different round surface. Three kittens always bring mittens to mind. On the stool pictured at left, one kitty loses mittens, one finds mittens and one dirties mittens; then the clean mittens are hung to dry around the seat.

I haven't figured out why they have mittens at all, let alone in the springtime with butterflies in the air! But that's the fun of being an artist. You can paint it any way you want.

10

Silent Night

Can the animals really talk on Christmas Eve? And does finding

a bird's nest in your Christmas tree really bring good luck in the

coming year? I'd like to think so, wouldn't you?

What You'll Need

- Wood sleigh from Cabin Crafters (approximate size 22″ × 14″)
- Wood preparation and finishing materials, including gesso
- Base-coating materials
- Deep blue-grey acrylic paint for base coat
- Deep blue-black acrylic paint for glazing
- Glazing (or gel) medium
- Krylon #1311 Matte Finishing Spray
- Mechanical pencil or stylus
- Tracing paper
- Transfer paper—grey and white
- Angled brush and white acrylic paint for undercoating
- White, black and sap green acrylic paint for pine needles
- X-Acto knife
- Scotch Magic Tape
- #0000 synthetic steel wool pad or piece of brown paper bag
- Q-tips and soft paper towels
- Cotton balls, silk (or nylon) squares and twisty ties
- Snow spattering tool (optional)
- Brushes—tiny round hair, small bright hair, medium bright hair, small bristle round, medium bristle round, large bristle round, small filbert rake, small mop, mops or large blending brushes of choice for glazing, large flat synthetic-hair brush for pine needles

OIL SUPPLIES
Gel medium, odorless thinner, white, Ivory Black, Raw Umber, Cadmium Yellow Light, Burnt Sienna, Sap Green, Vermilion Permanent, Prussian Blue. Mix these colors: pink, fawn, dark grey, basic green, dark brown (soft brown with more Raw Umber to deepen it).

ACRYLIC SUPPLIES
Gel medium, water, floating medium (optional), white, Pure Black, Raw Umber, Medium Yellow, Burnt Sienna, True Burgundy, Hauser Green Dark, Sap Green, Red Light, Prussian Blue. Mix these colors: pink, fawn, dark grey, basic green, dark brown (soft brown with less yellow so it is deeper).

Preparing Your Sleigh

Sand and prepare your sleigh with care. This is an elaborate project that deserves your best effort from the start. Gesso the bentwood front of the sleigh. Base-coat with several coats of deep blue-grey, lightly sanding or smoothing with a piece of brown paper bag between coats.

Glaze the Sleigh

1 Glaze the sleigh with deep blue-black. The starlit scene at one end should be very dark.

Choose a method of glazing with which you feel comfortable. You may glaze with acrylic paint and glazing mediums even if you'll be painting in oil, or you may glaze with gel and paint.

Blend and shade paint with mops or blending brushes of your choice. One of my favorite tools for applying, removing and blending paint is a "silk ball." (Wrap three or four cotton balls in a piece of silk or nylon hose and secure it with a twisty tie.) It is truly an amazing tool! Spray the sleigh with a protective coat of Krylon #1311 Matte Finishing Spray.

This pattern may be hand-traced or photocopied for personal use only. Enlarge at 154% to bring it up to full size.

This pattern may be hand-traced or photocopied for personal use only. Enlarge at 143% to bring it up to full size.

Undercoat the Design

 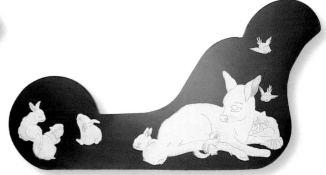

2 Trace the pattern and transfer the design outline with white transfer paper. Undercoat the design with white acrylic paint. The undercoat should be opaque in areas of white fur or areas that will be heavily glowed. Use an angled brush, and feather the fur edges as you work. Smooth the paint with a synthetic steel wool pad or a piece of brown paper bag.

3 Transfer the interior pattern of the design with grey transfer paper. Gel and paint pink in the ears. Lift out some paint toward the tips of the ears with a Q-tip. Blend in some white paint for more highlighting.

Be Prepared

Plan ahead how much of any animal you'll be working on at one time. This is a large project, and you'll rarely be working on a whole animal at once, let alone all of them at once. When planning, take into consideration your expertise, your speed and the open time of your medium. Get ready to flip pages as you progress on one part of an animal to finished fur, then backtrack and begin again on the next part.

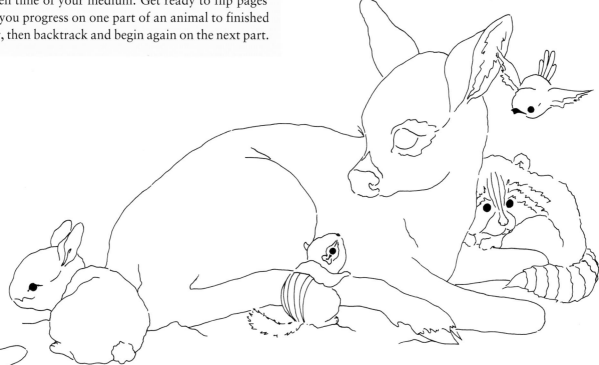

This pattern may be hand-traced or photocopied for personal use only. Enlarge at 159% to bring it up to full size.

Paint the Darks and Shadows

4 *Gel all surface areas you are painting.* Paint the black mask of the raccoon using the raccoons in Project 7 (page 81) to guide you. Paint other shadow areas in black, and begin the dark tail rings. Paint heavy white paint in white fur areas.

Proceed to step 7.

5 *Gel all surface areas you are painting.* Begin the squirrel with dark black shadow areas. As the brush unloads, paint the lighter, transparent-looking strokes.

Proceed to step 7.

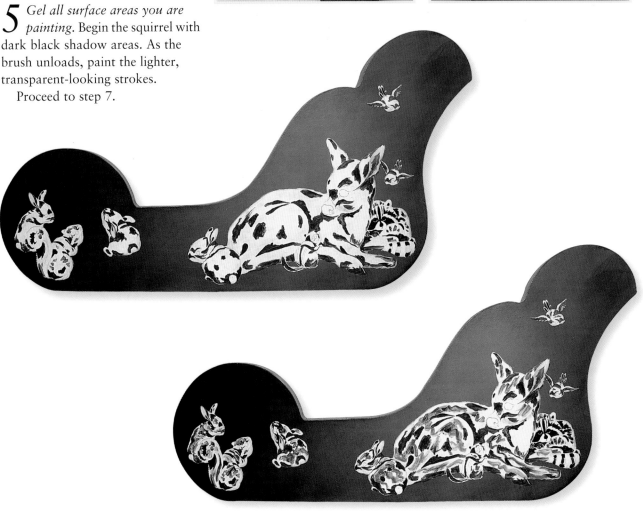

6 *Gel all surface areas you are painting.* All the other animals and birds have dark brown shadow areas. Even though the strokes look messy, they must be painted accurately, since these are the strokes that define the animals' shapes. Be particularly alert to negative shapes (such as a hip or jaw) that you create as you paint a brown shadow. Observe the shadow behind the fawn's hip. One edge of the stroke defines the shape of the hip and is very important. The other side of the stroke will be blended into the shadow and is of less concern.

7 With a light load of dark brown in your brush, loosely squiggle some of the paint into the gelled surface. The result will be a transparent brown. Take note of the amount of undercoat that should still be visible.

Add Fawn and Other Colors

8 The raccoon and squirrel have no fawn color. The two starlit bunnies have fawn only on their heads. Scrumble fawn loosely over the other animals and birds. Let the paint fall from the heavily loaded brush so as not to disturb the underlying colors or gel.

Don't panic! You really have to look, but your baby animals are still in there.

9 Use a heavily loaded brush to paint the remaining colors. The object is to float some color atop the existing paint without stirring it up.

Add Burnt Sienna to the fawn, chipmunk and birdlets in the areas that look "reddest" in the finished painting. Float yellow over the Burnt Sienna on the birdlets.

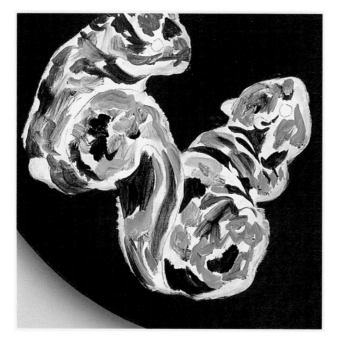

10 Scrumble dark grey over the squirrel.

The Fur Pattern

11 As you compare the fur diagram to the rough-brush photos on these two pages, notice that the squirrel, chipmunk and raccoon all have fairly similar fur: short, dense and fluffy on the body and long and fluffy on the tails. Note the even rotation of angles around the squirrel's tail.

Notice the sweep of the fur away from the fawn's nose. Imagine the nose pointed toward the sky, and then envision how the fur grows from the tip of the nose down to the extremities. Observe the fur growing down the legs out to the hooves, even as the legs turn.

Rough-Brush the Fur

Use an appropriate-size bristle brush for each animal. Begin brushing the edge fur of an area, then proceed to layer the fur within that area. Use a back-and-forth stroke and no pressure. Pressure on the brush will only mush the paint or scoop it off the surface. Wipe clean and re-gel your brush often to prevent excessive traveling of color.

12 Perfect the edge fur with a filbert rake. Very dark backgrounds can present two problems with edge fur: either you can't see the dark fur against the background, or the white undercoat demarcation shows. The solution: Add edge fur with white paint and a filbert rake. You may then simply blend in the roots of the white or gently lay darker fur on top of the white.

Bunnies, Birdlets and Raccoon

If you wish more detailed instructions for finishing the bunnies and birdlets, refer to Project 5 (page 65). The animals are larger and darker in this project but are essentially the same. For guidance in finishing the raccoon's face, paws and fur, turn to Project 7 (page 83).

Brush and Adjust Fur

13 Very dark markings can be painted and brushed simultaneously with paint in the bristle brush.

14 Continue brushing and adjusting until all your animals have good, strong color and well-defined form. They look a bit as if they've been frolicking in the dirt and brambles, but at least they're recognizable now.

Glow Some Areas

15 Soften the brown ear canals with a dry Q-tip. Then begin to glow and re-brush one or two areas at a time on your rough-brushed animal. Begin with large, distinct glows such as foreheads or hips. Once these are done, the others are more manageable.

16 The majority of glowing should be done with a dry Q-tip. In very large or bright glow areas, such as the fawn's hip, lift out a secondary glow with a wet Q-tip in the middle of the dry Q-tip glow.

17 For tiny glows, use a wet small bright brush. As you lift out glow areas, think about how the light is falling on the animals. Are you depicting an overall diffused light, or is there a definite light source (such as the star over the bunnies and squirrel) that will require bright wet glows where the light falls?

Re-Brush and Groom

18 Re-brush your glowed areas with a bristle brush, no pressure and a back-and-forth stroke. Wipe clean and re-gel your brush often to create smooth transitions of color in the glowed area.

For very bright glows, keep the brush from ever touching the bright white center. For hazier glows, allow paint to travel into the center. Vary the intensity of your glows to prevent a polka-dot composition.

Some areas will need to be glowed and re-brushed repeatedly until perfect fur emerges.

Add gelled Burnt Sienna to areas in which the fur needs to be redder. In some of the glowed areas, a bit of white and pink blended in with your bristle brush will give soft variation.

Paint and brush white fur in the muzzles, ears and breasts with a bristle brush or a filbert rake. Blend in pink for a babyish look. Use a small filbert rake to paint and brush white fur around the eyes.

19 (Left) Grey fur needs more glowing, re-brushing and color adjustments than brown fur. Just keep fiddling with it. Paint and extend final tail hairs with a filbert rake.

20 (Right) Paint delicate white fur in the fawn's ears with a filbert rake. Airplane the brush for wispy tips.

21 (Left) Lift out varying sizes of spots with a wet medium bright brush. Gently brush the spots with a bristle brush. Leave prominent spots bright in the middle. Tone down other spots by brushing through the entire spot.

22 (Right) Paint the fawn's hoof dark brown. Glow the hoof and then paint the fur back over the hoof with a filbert rake.

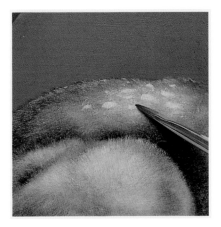

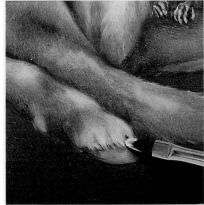

Finishing Your Animals

23 Paint the chipmunk's eye and black-and-white markings. Use deep paint on the markings and then brush them with a clean filbert rake. Add tiny whiskers with an X-Acto knife.

24 Give your squirrel a bright eye, whisker dots and twitchy whiskers. Perfect the tiny paws.

Paint the Fawn's Features

Large, luminous eyes are essential to a fawn's beauty. Really stretch yourself here and give it your very best effort!

↑ Begin with Raw Umber

↑ Add black and stretch the paint to the shape's edge

↑ Glow with a dry Q-tip

↑ Paint a black pupil, eyelashes and nostrils

↑ Lift out with a wet brush and blend

↑ Finish with sparkling white highlights

Painting the Wintry Woodland: Snowy Pine Needles

This technique works best with acrylic paint. If you painted the design in oil, pine needles that are over the fawn's body must also be painted in oil. The rest may be acrylic. Experiment with several brushes, because some work much better than others.

25 Heavily load a large, well-chiseled flat or bright brush with Sap Green, then dip one corner in black and the other corner in white. Stroke the brush on the palette until the colors gradually blend across the brush. Allow some white to remain relatively unblended on the "snow" side.

26 Gently bend the sides of the brush against a clean part of the palette. This will curve the edge of the chisel and allow you to create very "springy" bowed pine needles.

27 With the brush held almost perpendicular to the surface, gently press *only the chisel edge* of the brush on the surface, and then lift. Rotate the "snow" end and press again. Continue pressing on needles in clusters, adding white paint to your brush as the "snow" runs out. Occasionally, totally re-load the brush.

28 Begin with the needles farthest away from your eye. Subsequently layer needles with tips over the previous layer's "roots," just like fur!

For an even more realistic look, try glazing areas of the needles to create deep shadows and a spectrum of hues and values.

Paint Glistening Snow

Roughly paint white snowdrifts around your baby animals; then use these techniques to perfect them.

29 Wrap a Q-tip in a bit of silk or nylon. It's a versatile tool for blending or lifting out paint.

30 Load a bristle brush with white paint and stipple on bright, powdery drifts. (This is a good method to use on the runners, also.)

31 Make a small silk ball to lift out paths or to haze snow into the horizon.

Create a Fluffy Flurry

A combination of techniques helps control the storm.

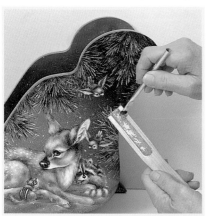

32 (Left) Spatter the entire sleigh using a spattering tool, a toothbrush or a bristle brush flipped against a knife. Spatter heavy "drifts" in the sleigh, the seat and the floor corners.

33 (Right) To adjust the composition of the spattered snow, randomly enlarge some of the flakes with a brush. You can also paint in some new flakes.

34 (Left) Lightly press your finger on a flake to enlarge and "fluff" it.

35 (Right) Paint that's left on your finger after you've pressed on a flake will make more flakes. Watch the flakes get paler as you repeatedly press a finger with only residual paint on it.

Final Touches

You may wish to repeat the scene on the other side of the sleigh or simply paint a quiet wilderness with no animals.

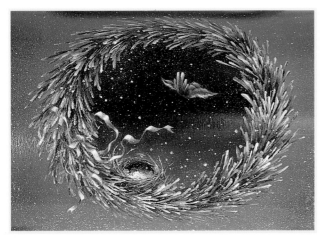

36 Paint the wreath on the front of the sleigh using techniques you've learned throughout this book.

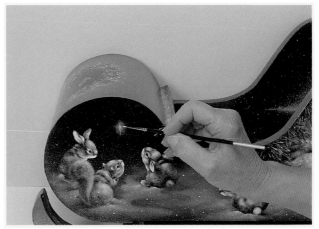

37 Save the star to paint last. Haze a dot of white paint with a silk-wrapped Q-tip. Pull out a few beams from the center with a tiny brush.

Re-load your brush, take a deep breath and let a single glimmering droplet of white fall from the brush onto the center of your star. All is calm, all is bright; sleep in heavenly peace!

Once all the painting is complete, bring out the beauty of your sleigh with satin varnish and finishing wax. Remember, to preserve the delicate fur lines, do not sand between the first and second coats of varnish.

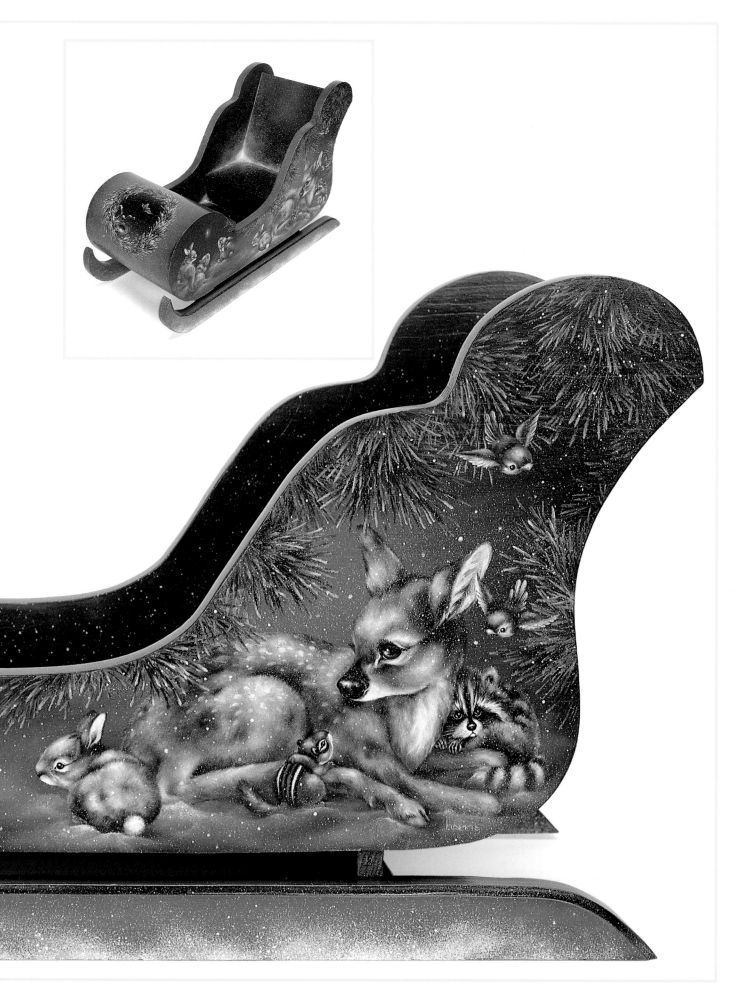

OOPS! NOW WHAT?

Not to worry, that's what! Even the most experienced of us mess up, change our minds or just want our paintings to look better. Here are some tips for no-fail painting!

Undercoat Ghosts

The Problem: Like an apparition, the undercoat keeps showing through the edge fur, especially if the background color is dark.

The Solution: Lift out your edge fur and repaint it in white paint with a filbert rake. Re-load the rake with the original fur color and, using a feather touch, stroke new fur on top of the wet white fur.

Race Against Time

The Problem: Everything was going swimmingly until your paint started drying up.

The Solution: Let it dry even more. Continuing to work now and trying to brush fur will only cause "lift" holes in the fur. After the paint is really dry, re-gel the area and blend in new fur; or, smooth the old paint with a synthetic steel wool pad, undercoat the area again, and start over.

Tracing Line Trauma

The Problem: Try as you might to keep them light, you can still see those lines!

The Solution: First, know your transfer papers—which ones will erase, which will lift with water, which will lift with thinner and which you'll never buy again! If all else fails, try these tricks. On edges, paint just shy of the lines and remove them when the painting is dry. Or, paint exactly up to and on the line, never over it. Often, even white paint will appear to cover the line, especially if a bit of shading is painted at the very edge. Or try lifting off the paint and covering the line with white acrylic paint. Then begin again.

Where's the Paint?

The Problem: You're painting the paint pattern, but all the strokes look transparent.

The Solution: Maybe you've too much gel on your surface and you should blot some off. More likely, you need to ease up on your pressure so as not to mix the paint and gel as you stroke. Let the paint fall off a heavily loaded brush.

Bad Dye Job

The Problem: Your animal is way too dark! You painted perfect strokes, but the paint was just too deep, especially the dark colors.

The Solution: This one's easy! Partially remove paint with a dry Q-tip—here, there and everywhere. Re-brush with gel in your brush, and like magic, it's fixed!

Haircut Time!

The Problem: Your animal is too fuzzy and she's "growing." Probably it happened before you knew it because you were watching where the brush had been, not where it was going.

The Solution: Use a wet lift-out brush as "clippers" and shear the fur. Then re-brush the tips.

Washed-Out Woes

The Problem: Your animal looks bleached. Perhaps there wasn't enough paint before you brushed, or perhaps you scooped it off or used too much gel as you brushed—whatever.

The Solution: Just add more paint now and re-brush. No problem!

Blow-Dry and Style

The Problem: Brylcreem baby just walked in. The angle of the fur to the body is too shallow and the hairs are too long and curved.

The Solution: Fluff him up. Re-brush the edges with "popped-up" fur. Adjust the interior fur, shortening and re-angling the layers as you brush.

Bad Hair Day

The Problem: You've brushed, you've fiddled, you've brushed again, and your animal still looks scruffy!

The Solution: Keep brushing. Dry-glow and add paint if your color is weakening. Ease up on your pressure. Better, but still not great? Dust the fur with a fluffy dry mop. What a difference!

Ring Around the Baby

The Problem: Everything is looking good, except your animal has a snowplowed ring of paint around it.

The Solution: Drag the ring back into the fur with a bristle brush, wiping the brush clean after each stroke. It's an easy fix, but next time, use less pressure and airplane the brush rather than skidding to a stop.

Monochromatic Mishap

The Problem: Where did all the colors go? Suddenly your animal is only one color.

The Solution: Lift out some areas with a dry Q-tip. Brush in new colors with paint in a gelled bristle brush. After this, clean your brush more frequently, ease up on your pressure and brush from light areas to dark rather than dark to light.

Wrong-Color Crisis

The Problem: One of your colors got away from you in the paint pattern, and now it won't go away in the rough brush.

The Solution: Quick and simple. Eliminate the offender with a Q-tip and re-brush.

"Help, I've Created a Monster!"

No fooling! Well, calm down. It will take a bit of redoing, but even this can be fixed. First, let's go over what went wrong.

The Problem: *Careless painting* of dark shadows, bad negative shapes (neck wrinkle, hip and ear), too much paint (width of strokes and overall depth of paint) and hairlining outside the lines (nose and paw) got you off to a shaky start.

Careless brushing magnified the problem. Common mistakes seen here include too much gel, fur brushed out too long (all over), wrong fur directions (face and tail), bad rotation of fur (hip and tail) and uneven brushing of edge fur (all over).

The Solution: Lift out stray edge fur and clean up nose, ear, muzzle and stripe shapes with a wet bright brush. Lift out excess paint in the fur with a dry Q-tip. Re-brush the fur, being more particular about even edges, length and rotation angles. Next time, you'll paint and brush more deliberately. Experience is a great teacher!

Case of the Disappearing Glow

The Problem:
You pulled too much paint into the area to begin with, or you didn't clean your brush often enough as you brushed, and your glow has vanished.

The Solution:
Not a big deal. Just glow and re-brush again. It happens all the time!

Slip-Sliding Away

The Problem:
What happened to the hair marks? Now you see them, now you don't!

The Solution:
Use more gel in your bristle brush to stabilize the marks and keep them from floating away in the water or thinner on the glow area.

Flood Control

The Problem: You were painting the perfect eye highlight (or other final detail), and suddenly the whole area is awash with water or thinner.

The Solution: Blot up the mess with a dry Q-tip and paint it again. The cause was excess water or thinner flowing down the handle or out of the ferrule of the brush. The way to prevent this is to keep the handle and ferrule out of the thinner or water when painting.

The Background Botch-Up

The Problem: Oh bother! Where did that come from? You scrupulously cleaned off straying paint smudges as you worked. Now your project is dry and you find another one!

The Solution: Oil paint can often be dry to the touch, but still removable with thinner or brush cleaner and a Q-tip. Acrylic paint can be removed with a Q-tip and rubbing alcohol, but go gently or you'll lift your background or base coat also. It's a good idea to always keep a small bottle of repair paint until after the project is finished.

Extra! Extra!

We really do learn from our mistakes. The wonderful thing about this method of painting fur and feathers is that almost anything can be fixed on the spot. Because you are solving problems as you go, one animal in one project can teach you more than you'd learn painting ten projects in a less forgiving technique. If you can fix or improve something, no matter how small, do it. You'll be amazed how rapidly your eye, and therefore your art, improves!

SUPPLIERS

PAINTING SURFACES

Allen's Woodcrafts
3020 Dogwood Lane
Sapulpa, OK 74066
(918) 224-8796
Fax (918) 224-3208

Designs by Bentwood, Inc.
PO Box 1676
Thomasville, GA 31799
(912) 226-1223

Cabin Crafters
1225 W. First Street
Nevada, IA 50201
(800) 669-3920
Fax (515) 382-3106

Cabin Craft Southwest, Inc.
1500 Westpark Way
Euless, TX 76040
(800) 877-1515
Fax (817) 571-4925

Cape Cod Cooperage
1150 Queen Anne Road
Chatham, MA 02633
(508) 432-0788
Fax (508) 430-0317

Crews' Country Pleasures
HCR 64, Box 53
Thayer, MO 65791
(417) 264-7246
Fax (417) 264-3889

Drake Distributors
PO Box 69
Cottondale, AL 35453
(800) 888-8653

Pesky Bear
5059 Roszyk Hill Road
Machias, NY 14101
Tel/Fax (716) 942-3250

Walnut Hollow Farm, Inc.
1409 State Road 23
Dodgeville, WI 53533-2112
Available from craft stores nationwide, or for buying information, call
(800) 950-5101

MATERIALS

Silver Brush Limited
P.O. Box 414
Windsor Industrial Park, #18E
91 North Main Street
Windsor, NJ 08561-0414
(609) 443-4900
Fax (609) 443-4888
E-mail: BrushLady@aol.com

Martin/F. Weber Company
2727 Southampton Road
Philadelphia, PA 19154
(215) 677-5600
Fax (215) 677-3336

Plaid Enterprises, Inc. (FolkArt)
P.O. Box 7600
1649 International Court
Norcross, GA 30091-7600
(770) 923-8200
Fax (770) 381-6705

INDEX